learning
about
NATURE
through
CRAFTS

learning about NATURE through CRAFTS

by Virginia W. Musselman

STACKPOLE BOOKS

This book is dedicated to
MARGUERITE ICKIS
Long-time friend, generous with time and interest

Price: $3.95
Standard Book Number: 8117-0938-8
Library of Congress Catalog Card Number: 78-85646
Printed in U.S.A.

CONTENTS

Guide to the
157 Craft Projects

Guide to Using Nature's Things in Crafts

9

Introduction

This book is a companion piece to LEARNING ABOUT NATURE THROUGH GAMES (Stackpole, 1967). In many ways it may be considered a progression of that book, which was designed to help parents and leaders to lead a child to use his own five senses in enjoying nature, and emphasized looking and finding. This book emphasizes what to do with what is found.

Psychologists tell us that early stimulation is highly important in a child's mental development; that children learn more quickly when they know the *names* of things; that activities can be very simple, require no expensive materials, yet be fun; and that when parents or other adults share the experiences, children are quick to respond.

Many adults know very little about the world of nature. Many are not highly skilled in crafts. Anyone, however, can develop a curiosity about what he or she sees on walks and trips, a willingness to learn *something* about it, an enjoyment in talking about it, and a moderate ability to use nature's storehouse of materials and supplies in making simple craft projects.

The *making* in this book is only part of the adult-child process of learning together. It is a result rather than a reason. The finished product may be pretty, or useful, or amusing, or experimental, or just-for-fun. The most important result is not the object made, but the enjoyment of finding out and talking about the materials being used—together.

For example, turning pinecones into bird feeders, or Christmas wreaths, or a Thanksgiving turkey is only a part of the real project. If it is combined with the fun of finding, collecting and identifying those cones, seeing the blue sky through the pine tree, watching a squirrel on a branch, walking on the springy pine needles under the tree, smelling them, identifying the tree by the number of needles in each little "bundle"—these are what give the real *meaning* to the craft project.

And the more that is learned and talked about, the more appreciation and interest develop. What are pine trees used for? What do their seeds look like? Where do they grow? Were they here when the early colonists arrived? All such questions go much further in arousing the child's interest than if the craft project were made for itself alone, without the additional stimulation of shared discussion and information.

This book is not written for parents or leaders who are trained naturalists or craft specialists. It is written for the average, everyday parent or adult who knows very little about nature or crafts, but who is interested in learning enough to stimulate a child's interest and to satisfy some of the child's natural curiosity. Perhaps it will open doors for both, so that both may go further into the wonderful world of nature by learning a bit more about it. Many excellent books on nature and nature crafts already exist and can help the adult and child go on with a new, absorbing hobby. This book is meant to provide a short, first step on that journey.

The examples used are only a few and should be regarded as only a sampling, an example of how such material can be used. It is easily supplemented by the many other books covering the various fields of plant and animal life. The building of a simple nature library can be a shared project for both parent and child, providing a sharing of interests and enjoyment. Neither has to be an expert, but both can develop a liking for, and appreciation of, the wonderful world of nature. Games will help. Crafts will help. Books, magazines, pictures, photographs, films and other media all help. Most of all, the sympathetic sharing of interests between adult and child brings the greatest rewards to each.

Credits... and Thanks

Many of the nature crafts in this book come from my active days in camp and playground work. Some were developed by other playground leaders in public recreation agencies. Some were described to me by friends and relatives. I wish that individual credit could be given to all these sources.

Special credit should go to the National Recreation Association, now the National Recreation and Park Association, for which I was Program Director for many years. This gave me the opportunity of meeting with, and learning from, many leaders in recreation throughout the country.

My special thanks should go, too, to Ruth and "Wink" Tapply, of the Office of Community Recreation Service of the State of New Hampshire, for their generosity in sharing their skills with me.

Useful Supplies, Tools and Equipment

String-Savers' Specials

Nobody will ever need *all* of these, but at some time or other any item in this short listing may be useful. Just keep an eye open for useable throw-aways. Think up ways to use them. They'll save your dishes, pots, pans and other less expendable items. Useful throw-aways can include such items as:

Ice cream, cottage cheese and other cartons, all sizes, washed and dried. They make excellent containers for small cones, berries, nuts, seeds, pebbles, sand, and other such craft items as bits of wire, tacks, and the like.

Ice cream and lollipop sticks and spoons are wonderful for mixing paints, for making bases for shell figures, and for many small projects of wood.

Foil pans, all sizes and shapes. They make good containers for paint or other liquids. They also make good storage and work trays.

Egg cartons. The plastic-coated ones are great for small amounts of paint or other liquids. The cardboard ones make good display trays for rocks and pebbles.

Oilcloth and plastic cloths. Invaluable to save table tops and floors from messy spills.

Felt scraps. Useful for leaf printing, covering the backs of wreaths and other articles that might scratch a table or door. Useful for tiny caps for woodland creatures, and backings for nut and cone jewelry.

Shelf paper. Excellent for fingerpainting, and much less expensive than special fingerpaint paper. Use the glossy side.

Corks, all sizes and shapes. They make attractive bases for small models, backings for jewelry. Save the thin ones from inside bottle caps as well as the fatter ones. Cork combines well with wood and leather, since it, too, is a natural material.

Wire, both copper and galvanized, different weights. Invaluable for holding natural materials like cones, twigs, nuts, and the like in place, for hanging shadow frames, wreaths and pictures, and for all sorts of uses for binding and tying.

Cardboard, corrugated paper. Fine for backings, mountings for prints, work sheets and other uses.

Newspapers. Lots of them. They make good working surfaces and pads.

Sponges. They make good paint dabbers as well as mop-ups for spills.

Mailing tubes. Useful for making armatures for modeled figures. Also for pin-point telescope.

Paper. All kinds. Construction paper, typing paper, newsprint are all excellent for making prints, drawing, painting, and many other types of projects.

Boxes. Suitboxes and shoeboxes are fine for storing dried natural materials until used, and for separating different types. Also for dioramas.

String and cord. Always useful for tying, for hanging things up to dry. Cotton, nylon, jute, and leather thongs can all be used.

Muffin tins, tin or foil. They make good containers for seeds, and for all kinds of paints.

Waxed or plastic milk cartons. A two-quart size makes a fine "vasculum", or plant carrier, when collecting live plant specimens. Cut a lid in one side and put enough water into the carton to keep the roots moist.

Tin cans. The small, frozen fruit juice ones are useful for storing small items, or small amounts of paint. The larger, coffee-can size are often nicely marked to show graduated amount of contents. Larger cans are useful for making plaster of paris because they can be discarded afterwards.

Tools and Equipment

Again, no one will need or use all of these, but most of them come in handy from time to time. Most of them are usually available in home workshops.

14

Spray cans of paints. These save lots of time and can be used, with a bit of practice, by children if the spraying area is well-protected by newspapers or plastic cloths. Most types of paint, including gold, silver and bronze are now available in spray cans. The new acrylic paints can be thinned with water, but look like oil paints.

Hobby shop paints. These are the very handy, very small bottles of paint used on model airplanes. They are inexpensive, save storage space, and make it unnecessary to buy more paint than is needed.

Brushes, assorted sizes, for water-soluble and oil paints, and for varnish, shellac and lacquer.

Crayons. Collect both wax and pastel types.

Sandpaper, assorted grades. Its use will give a finished look to many projects.

Knives. A really good penknife will be very useful. Also various paring knives. Keep them sharp.

Scissors and shears. Don't use good dressmaker shears for nature projects! Kitchen ones, and tin snips are much better.

Hammer, not too heavy for easy use by a child.

Coping saw and blades, for cutting cones and other nature materials.

Cross-cut saw, for other saw jobs.

Nails and tacks, assorted sizes. Keep in small cans or bottles.

Tape, both transparent and masking. Very useful sometimes in place of glue or nails.

Rubber cement. Very clean and handy for paper and felt.

Glue. Elmer's and Sobo are both very good.

Pliers. Better than fingers when handling wire.

Ruler. The eighteen-inch length is the most useful.

Turpentine and lacquer thinner. Good for cleaning brushes as well as thinning. It is hard to remember what to use with what! Here's a reminder:

Paint	*Cleaner and thinner*
Showcard and poster	Water
Enamel	Turpentine
Lacquer	Lacquer thinner
Oil Paints	Turpentine or linseed oil
Printer's Ink	Turpentine
Shellac	Alcohol
Gilt Powders	Banana oil
Varnish	Turpentine or linseed oil
Acrylic	Water

Work gloves. They may be clumsy, but they'll save wear and tear on the hands. Important when bending wire, cutting tin or hardware cloth, or when handling prickly, natural materials such as burs, tumbleweed, thistles, and the like.

Plaster of paris. Very popular for making casts of leaves, animal prints and other objects. Also for bases, and plaques.

There is a right way to mix plaster of paris to get the best results when making casts of footprints or other objects. Children are always amazed to see what looks like thick cream turn into a hard substance. It can even be carved.

Plaster of paris is calcium sulphate made by heating or oxidizing gypsum, a mineral. When mixed with water it generates heat, then hardens very quickly.

Equipment and supplies needed are few:

A cup for measuring the water
A cup of equal size for measuring the plaster
A disposable container for mixing the plaster and water
Mixing stick, also disposable
Plaster of paris
Water

Estimate the amount of mixed plaster needed for the job. Measure this amount of water into the container. Measure the plaster of paris, *twice the amount of the water.* Then, *pour the plaster into the water.* Allow the plaster to settle on the bottom a few minutes, then stir slowly and thoroughly until the mixture is smooth. It is then ready to pour and harden.

Plan ahead. Prepare the mold or plan the project before mixing the plaster of paris, because it hardens quickly and must be used at once. Measure carefully. Don't try to add more water. It won't work out right. Measure the plaster with a dry cup. Use a disposable container and mixing stick because plaster is almost impossible to remove once it has hardened. Milk cartons or tin cans make good containers. They should be big enough to hold three times the amount of water needed. Make sure the container is large enough. AND—never pour liquid plaster down a drain!

16

PART I

Crafts From
Nature's Tree Trimmings

Something To Look For

Trees

There they are, in every section of the country, in almost every park, on most schoolyards and playgrounds, on city streets, and in the yards of private homes. They are all around us, but all too often not recognized by name as all familiar friends should be. With trees, like people, we often have to say, "Your face is familiar, but I can't remember your name."

The United States has over a thousand species of native trees—to Europe's hundred! Nobody is likely to know all of them. The ones most often found across the country should be like old friends, however, familiar, enjoyed and loved.

Our varied climate and geography account for the wide variety of species. Some are native to, or will grow only in certain sections in which the climate and geography are most suitable. The palms, eucalyptus, bald cypress, redwoods and madrone are a few of these. In our mobility of travel, many trees that are strangers in our region can be seen in their native areas as we visit that part of the country. Some can be seen locally in special botanical gardens and arboretums.

Trees belong in two big families, the evergreens and the broadleaf trees. Both families provide nature tree trimmings for craft projects.

17

The Evergreens. Most of these bear cones of some sort, have needles in place of leaves, and keep the needles. A few species, including the larch, tamarack and bald cypress, lose their needles in the winter. Different species of evergreens grow in most of the United States. They may be identified by their needles and their cones, as well as the bark, and flowers.

The Broadleaved Trees. Most of these lose their leaves in the winter. Many of them provide the beautiful fall colors in their foliage. Their leaves and fruits often provide natural materials for projects.

Among the best known of the broadleaved trees are many favorites such as oak, maple, birch, beech, aspen, willow, elm, sycamore, ash, walnut, hickory, gum, cottonwood, pecan, horse chestnut, dogwood, magnolia, poplar, apple, osage orange, pear, cherry and other fruit trees. Many are valuable for their wood for many uses; some for their decorative flowers, leaves or fruit; some for their fruits for food; some for their shape and shade; others for many other reasons.

Some of these trees are part of the environment of all of us. As such, they deserve more of our attention, familiarity and appreciation. Collecting and using their "tree trimmings" is one way to develop this—not just to make things, but to become more observant and knowledgeable of our friends and neighbors, TREES.

In doing this, we may also come to know and to enjoy certain tree-users, the birds. They, too, are a form of "tree trimming". Luring them closer for our enjoyment will be made easier by providing birdhouses, feeders, and a water supply. Here, too, are good nature projects.

Tree Trimmings

Nature materials will vary widely in different sections of the country, but look for—and collect—such tree trimmings as:

Acorns. Different sizes and shapes from different kinds of oak trees. Also their cups.

Apples. The small sizes work up best in projects. Lady apples are especially pretty for Della Robbia wreaths.

Beechnuts. Small but very pretty. They make good petals for flowers for placques.

Birch bark. Never tear off the bark from a living tree. Use the bark that has been discarded.

Bottle tree pods. Lovely in wreaths.

Catalpa pods. Children call them "Indian tobacco".

Cones. All the different species of cones from the conifers, from the tiny hemlock cones to the enormous cones of the longleaf pine.

Cypress pods from Italian cypress. A California variety.

18

Eucalyptus leaves. Different varieties have different shapes.

Eucalyptus pods. Some have big, fat, thimble-shaped pods. Other varieties have other sizes and shapes of pods.

Evergreen boughs and sprays. Use prunings.

Hickory Nuts. Whole or halved are both useful.

Holly leaves and berries. For lots of holiday decorations.

Horse chestnuts. The hulls and chestnuts are both useful.

Jacaranda pods. They look like little castanets.

Kumquats. For wreaths and holiday decorations.

Laurel and rhododendron leaves. Pretty for swags, wreaths.

Leaves. From any kind of tree. For prints, laminating, etc.

Lemons. For holiday decorations.

Locust pods. For making ornaments, figures, decorations.

Magnolia leaves. Handsome for decorations.

Manzanita. A desert shrub, or small tree. Branches and roots often have strange shapes.

Oranges. For holiday wreaths and swags.

Osage oranges. For holiday decorations and pomanders.

Palm fronds. Many uses. Can be split and woven, or made into holiday decorations and tree hangings.

Seeds. From peach, cherry and other fruit trees. Can be used to make necklaces, belts, and other articles.

Sycamore and plane tree balls. Use for holiday decorations.

Twigs. Use prunings.

Walnuts. Use for jewelry, beads, belts, etc.

Something To Talk About

Sharing wonder makes it more wonderful. Sharing interest and curiosity about trees and their "trimmings" helps the child and adult to really *see* the trees, not just accept them as part of the landscape. Putting wonder, interest and information into words intensifies the pleasure of sharing. But what to talk about?

What IS a Tree?

Trees are the largest living plants! They grow from seeds, just like other plants. For example, the acorn is the seed of the oak tree. Plant it and see!

The main stem of a tree is called the *trunk*. Find a tree stump and see what the inside of the trunk looks like. In the center are many rings making up a large section of the trunk called the *heartwood*. This is really deadwood, but it strengthens the trunk and helps to hold it erect. Because this wood is dead, trees can sometimes live and grow with big holes in their trunks.

Next to the heartwood in the center is layer after layer (depend-

19

ing upon the age of the tree), of *sapwood*. This carries water and other substances up into the leaves from the roots.

Between the sapwood and the bark is a layer called the *cambium,* made up of very important cells that are invisible to the naked eye but can be seen through a microscope. The cambium makes new sapwood on its inner side, and new bark on its outer side. It therefore controls the growth of the circumference of the tree and its branches, and thus produces the annual growth rings that enable us to find out how old the tree is.

Outside the cambium is the *inner bark*. It contains microscopic vessels that bring the food manufactured by the leaves down to other parts of the tree, including the roots.

The outer bark of a tree is mostly cork, and serves to protect the tree from insects, blows, loss of water by evaporation, and other hazards. The outer bark is constantly forming outward, and is finally discarded. Different trees lose their bark gradually in different ways. One of the most noticeable is the paper birch, with its long, bark curls. Another is the shagbark hickory, with its long strips of bark that fall off from time to time. Homeowners call such trees that shed their bark in long pieces "dirty" trees, because they litter the yard.

The leaves of a tree are its food factory. By very complex methods, the leaves absorb carbon dioxide from the air and give off oxygen, so necessary to animal life. They have cells that manufacture the green substance called *chlorophyl* which gives the leaves their green color. Through the action of the sun's rays, by a process still not completely understood, the rays of the sun are absorbed by the chlorophyl, and carbon, hydrogen and oxygen combine to form a sort of sugar. At night, when the sun's rays are gone, this sugar turns to starch. And so the leaves are like a real laboratory, making the food that supports the tree. That is why too much defoliation, by insects sometimes, can kill a tree.

Trees have thousands of leaves—and no two are exactly alike! Gather a number from the same tree and compare them!

Trees provide shade for small animals and tender plants that cannot stand the direct sun. As the tree and its leaves fall and decay humus is formed, necessary to plant and animal life. It is also highly important in preventing erosion because it is very absorbent. Trees give shelter and provide living quarters for birds and small animals. The relationship and interdependence of living things is called *ecology*.

Evergreens

These are the trees that have needles instead of leaves, bear cones, and in most cases stay green all winter. A few, such as the larch,

RED CEDAR

SPRUCE

WHITE PINE

Evergreens

tamarack and bald cypress, bear cones but drop their needles in the winter. Some form of evergreen tree is found in almost every section of the country. In fourteen states some type of evergreen has been declared the official state tree. Evergreens are very important in providing natural materials for nature craft projects. Often one variety can be substituted for another. Among the most well-known and often used are:

Pines. If the needles of the evergreen come in little "bundles", that tree is some type of pine. Counting the number of needles in the bundle is one very good way to identify the species.

The White Pine has five needles in the bundle, and they stay on the tree from three to five years. The needles are from three to five inches long and a lovely bluish green. The cones are from five to eight inches long. In the fall of their second year they open and let the winged seeds fall out. The bark of the white pine is almost black in color.

The Western White Pine has shorter and thicker needles that are from two to four inches long. Its cones are so long and thin that they are sometimes called "finger cones".

In Colonial times, the finest white pines were considered the property of the English king and were branded with his mark, usually a big R for Rex or a broad arrow. No one could cut down these trees except the king's men, and they were used for masts for the royal navy. This ban was one of the laws that the Americans bitterly resented.

The Red or Norway Pine has needles from four to six inches long, in bundles of two. The needles are very sharp and pointed. The cone is light brown in color, cone-shaped, and about two inches long. The cones have no stalks, and their scales, or "petals", are smooth, not pointed as the scales of other pines are. The cones form high up in the tree every two to four years.

The Longleaf Pine is a southern tree. It has long, very flexible needles eight to eighteen inches in length, in bundles of three. These needles are often used in making mats, baskets and other woven objects. Its cones are huge—from five to ten inches long. These big cones make lovely holiday decorations and excellent birdfeeders.

21

The longleaf pine is a valuable pulp tree, and is also used for making paints, varnish, shoe polish, printing ink, and other turpentine and resin products.

Jack Pines have two needles in a bundle. They grow quickly along edges of fields. In Colonial days, the settlers thought that it was a witch tree, and that it was dangerous to get within ten feet of it. They also thought that it poisoned the soil.

The Cedars have tiny needles set around the stems. *Red Cedar* or *Juniper* has spiny needles, very sharp to the touch. *White Cedar*, or *Arborvitae* (tree of life), has scale-like needles.

White cedar got its name "Arborvitae" from a French king. A French expedition headed by Jacques Cartier wintered along the St. Lawrence. When it returned to France, it carried specimens of cedar, thus the first American tree was introduced into Europe. Members of the crew drank a tea made from cedar branches to cure their scurvy, a remedy they had learned from the Indians. The Indians called the tree Feather Heap because it made good tinder for fire-making by friction.

Cedar was the first American wood to be used in making pipe organs. It is said that Mittelberger first noticed its resonance by listening to rain drip on shingles.

The Spruces and Firs have medium length needles. Spruce needles are stiff, sharp, and four sided. Roll them between the fingers to feel those sides. Fir and balsam needles are flat, and won't roll. The cones of a spruce hang *down*. Those of the fir stand *upright* on the branch. This is one very good way to tell the difference between spruces and firs.

The spruce provides most of the pulp used to make newsprint. Its resin is the hiker's chewing gum. The Indians and early settlers used its long, slender, strong roots to sew birchbark into canoes, baskets, and other utensils. Squirrels and many varieties of birds love its seeds. Its wood is resonant and is sometimes used to make sounding boards for musical instruments.

Hemlocks were well-known to the early settlers. Their housewives made brooms from the branches. Indians pounded its inner bark between stones and made poultices for sores and wounds. Paper pulp is made from the Hemlock, and its bark is used for tanning leather.

The roots of the hemlock are so hard that they will nick a hatchet. When burned the wood throws off sparks and so was seldom used in tent or tepee. Birds eat its seeds. Deer graze on its lower branches. Small animals find winter refuge under its low, sweeping branches.

Its cones are very tiny, like little miniatures. They grow at the tips of the graceful sprays and are often used in making holiday and other decorations.

22

The Bald Cypress, native to southeastern United States, bears cones but loses its needles in the winter. It is one of the few trees that can live with its roots in mud and water. It has a strange way of sending up buttresses, called cypress "knees", that rise above the water, help to support the trunk, and provide air to the roots. These knees are solid wood and have a porous bark filled with air spaces. They are often used in making lamp bases, and for other craft projects.

Cypress trees are often draped with Spanish Moss, which is not a moss at all, but a plant without roots or broad leaves. The stems and very narrow leaves are covered with grey scales that protect the chlorophyl inside. The chlorophyl makes the food the plant needs from air and water. Spanish moss is not a parasite. It does not feed on the tree. It only lives there, high up in the air.

Redwoods and Sequoias are limited in number and geography, but they are trees that everyone hopes to—and should—see at some time in his or her life. Once seen, they will never be forgotten.

The Redwoods once covered most of the northern hemisphere before the glacial period. Now they are confined to a strip of land along the Pacific coast from the Chelco River in Oregon to Salmon Creek Canyon in California. With the Giant Sequoias, they are among the largest and oldest examples of life in North America. A redwood is the tallest tree. A Sequoia is the most massive.

The redwood may grow three hundred and fifty feet tall, with a diameter of from twenty to twenty-seven feet. The biggest example is called "Founder's Tree", at Garberville, California. It was three hundred and sixty-four feet tall in 1947. It is between three and four thousand years old, with bark a foot thick.

The bark and wood of a redwood contains a chemical that protects it from insects and fungus. Its needles are sharp-pointed, flat, very short, and a quarter to an inch long. They are set next to each other, and on twigs opposite each other, which gives them a feathery look. The cones are very small, egg-shaped, hard, and form at the ends of the branches. It takes a year for them to get an inch long. Then they open, and the tiny, numerous seeds fall out.

The wood is used for railroad ties, bridge supports, shingles, ceilings, doors, furniture, caskets and other articles that require a long-lasting wood.

The Giant Sequoias are among the oldest and most massive of all trees. They are found in groves of from five to a thousand in a small area in California. Their needles are bright green, like those of the Cedars. The cones are two to three inches long, and a dull, yellow-brown in color. The sap is a purple-red. Indians used to drink it in search of mystical powers, probably because of the trees' great size and age. The majesty of these enormous trees must be seen to be believed. They form a rich heritage for this nation, and their preservation and conservation is a national responsibility.

The Broadleaved Trees

These include the many familiar trees, most of which lose their leaves in the winter. A few, such as the magnolia and the holly, hold on to their leaves. Each section of the country has its own species of these deciduous trees native to it. Some species can be found, either native or cultivated, in almost every region. The oaks and maples are such trees.

Broadleaved trees can be identified by their leaves, fruits, flowers, and bark. Many supply natural materials for craft projects. The autumn colors of the leaves are another means of identification. Many of these trees are useful in industry, and have played a real part in the history of the nation. Among the most generally familiar trees are the following:

The Aspen, belonging to the Poplar family, is native to North America. It is found almost everywhere. It is the tree that springs up first in open fields or burned-over areas, or along the edges of the woods. Early trappers knew it well because bears often scratched it, and beavers used it to build their dams and for food. Westerners use it for corrals because the wood does not splinter. It is used to make berry boxes, too, because the wood has no odor and does not stain. It is also used to make excelsior for the same reason.

Its leaves are dark green on top, silvery underneath, and their long, flexible stems are attached to the boughs in a curious, hinge-like way. The slightest breeze sets them dancing, giving the tree a beautiful silvery shimmer as the undersides show. In the fall, the leaves turn a silvery yellow. Silver-gilt aspens growing up a mountainside in the Far West in the autumn are a very lovely sight.

Its scientific name, Populus Tremuloides, means "the trembling poplar". The Greeks said that it was like a woman's tongue, never still. The Onandaga Indians called it "noisy leaf".

There is a pretty little legend that the aspen was a witness to Christ's Crucifixion, and that the gentle tree was so distressed that it has quivered and trembled ever since.

The Beech is one of the most beautiful of the broadleaved trees. Its leaves are long, pointed, thin, crisp, with the feel of crisp taffeta. They turn a deep yellow in the fall, finally turn brown, and stay on the trees for a time, deep into winter. Its buds in early spring are like golden points on lances or spears. Its small beechnuts are popular with animals, ruffed grouse and other wildlife.

The trunk is very smooth, and a pale grey. It may reach a hundred feet in height. The wood is used for fuel, furniture, and other articles. Because of its smooth bark, the beech is sometimes

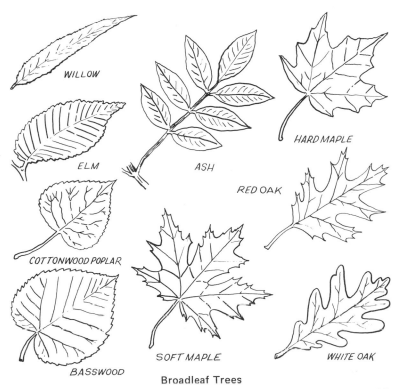

WILLOW

ELM

ASH

HARD MAPLE

RED OAK

COTTONWOOD POPLAR

SOFT MAPLE

WHITE OAK

BASSWOOD

Broadleaf Trees

called "the initial tree" and offers a real temptation to anyone with a penknife handy. Legend says that the beech is never struck by lightning.

The Birches can usually be identified by their bark, which is discarded in curls; sometimes small, sometimes in long shreds. The names for the various birches come from the colors of their bark. Birchbark curls will burn even when wet, and have helped many a camper to start a fire in the rain. The leaves are longish, have saw-like edges, and their leaf veins are opposite. The catkins grow upright just below the leaves, or between them, and droop as they get mature. Birch leaves are yellow in the fall.

The Canoe or Paper Birch is the easiest to recognize and the most romantic. It is the tree that supplied the Indians and early settlers with birchbark for their canoes, drinking cups, and cooking utensils. Its inner bark could be made into a flour. Its distinguishing characteristic is the startlingly white outer bark that develops some black streaks as the tree gets older.

Black Birch gets its name from the very dark bark of this tree. It is sometimes called Sweet or Cherry Birch because its twigs and bark are aromatic and sweet to the taste.

The Yellow Birch is one of the largest of the birches. Its bark is a greyish yellow—in fact, it is sometimes called the Grey Birch. The bark comes off in shreds and curls, making a very interesting design on the trunk.

The Red Birch droops almost like a willow, and can be found along the banks of streams throughout the eastern half of the U.S. Its bark is a reddish brown, and curls of it break off the trunk, as is usual with the birches.

The Cottonwood grows over most of the United States east of the Rockies. It grows very tall, sometimes a hundred and sixty feet. Its leaves are somewhat heart-shaped, come to a sharp point, and have sawtooth edges. Its flowers hang in long sprays in the spring, and when they fall the air looks as if a snowstorm had come by.

Legend says that the Indian discovered the design for his tepee by twisting a cottonwood leaf between his fingers. Indian children still make play tepees that way. Try it, and see what a fine tepee shape the leaf will make.

The Dogwood is native to many sections, and cultivated for its spring flowers in many others. Its family name, Cornus, means "horn", referring to the hardness of its wood. The wood is sometimes used for bobbins and shuttles. The Indians made a scarlet dye from its bark, and used it to decorate their blankets, feathers, belts and other objects. The bark of the tree looks a bit like alligator skin.

The flowers are white or pink, sometimes red in cultivated specimens. They are borne flat on the boughs, in a curious, tray-like way. What looks like white petals are really *bracts*. The flower is really the inconspicuous center of the dogwood's so-called flower. The red berries that form after the flowers are gone are very much relished by birds. A non-flowering variety of dogwood produces blue berries, also very popular with the birds.

Legend says that Christ's cross was made of a dogwood tree. It was so ashamed that Christ promised it that never again would it grow large enough to be so used. Ever since it has been a small tree. Its white petals each year show the rust marks of the nails of the cross. The center of the flower shows the crown of thorns, and its red berries signify the drops of blood that were caused by the crown of thorns.

The Elm. Its vase-like shape is familiar to Midwest and New England streets and fields. Early settlers soaked its bark overnight and pulled off long, flat strips to make chair bottoms. Its wood is very tough, heavy and hard to split.

The White Elm is the most familiar of the elm family. It grows into a magnificent tree. Its leaves are fairly small, oblong, slightly lopsided, serrated, with alternate veining. They turn a glowing yellow in the fall.

The Slippery Elm has an aromatic inner bark. Indians and early settlers used it to quench thirst, because its astringent quality stimulates the flow of saliva—as schoolchildren learn early when they unsuspectingly chew a twig. In early days it was also powdered and mixed with water to cure sore throats and fever.

The Eucalyptus tree was imported from Australia over a hundred years ago. Its name means "well-covered", because each little bud has a small cap that blows off when the flower is ready to bloom. The first eucalyptus tree in the United States was planted in San Francisco. Now there are millions of them growing in the West. They are used for windbreaks for citrus fruit orchards, sugar beet fields, cotton fields and other crops that can be injured by wind and cold.

It is one of the few trees that have different kinds of leaves on the same tree. They are different in size, color, shape, and texture. The leaves always have smooth edges, and some of them turn a dark red in the fall. The tree sheds all year round.

Seedpods vary in different species. Some are smooth, some are ribbed, some look like little caps, others like small cups.

The flowers, leaves, bark, buds and fruit all have an aromatic fragrance very noticeable after a rain. The bark sheds in long strips, giving the tree a mottled look.

The Hickory has compound leaves, meaning that its leaves are attached to one central stem. They turn yellow, then brown, and fall off early in the fall. The nuts of these trees are hard, fairly small, but delicious to both squirrels and humans. They are good for use in many craft projects, also. The wood of the hickory is very tough, resilient and shockproof. For these reasons it is used for making tool handles, wagon wheels, and other articles that must resist shock. Its wood is also split, bent, and woven into baskets. It is an important fuel wood, also, burning slowly with a hot fire. A cord of hickory is the equal of a ton of coal. Hickory makes good charcoal. Colonial housewives used its ashes in making soap.

The Shagbark Hickory gets its name from the way its bark comes loose and falls off in long strips, giving the tree trunk a shaggy look.

The Holly may get its name from the word "holy". Its history goes far back into the past, when it was supposed to have magic powers. Its use in holiday decorations is a remnant of these old superstitions.

It belongs to a family called Aquifoliaceae, "trees with needles in their leaves". Just feel the points of its leaves, and find out that the tree is well-named. Its leaves, bark and berries are poisonous to humans if eaten, because they contain ilicin, used medically in treating rheumatism. Birds, however, relish the berries.

Its wood is a lovely ivory-white, used often for wood carving because of its ivory-like look. It is also used for making musical instruments. The tree grows as a bush in cold sections, but makes a large tree in more temperate climates. In the East, and South, the leaves are a glossy, dark green. But on the West Coast the leaves are often variegated with white. Oregon holly is an important export for Christmas decorations.

The Maples, along with the Oaks, are among the most beautiful and useful trees in America and are found, native or cultivated, in almost every region. They are roughly divided into two main types, the hard maple and the soft maple, of which the hard maple is the more commercially useful. Their fruits are called *keys.* They are formed in pairs, like wings, with a seed in each wing. The keys are light in weight, and can be carried good distances by the wind.

The Sugar Maple is a hard maple. It can grow to be a hundred feet tall, with a beautiful, wide spread. Its leaves grow on long stems, have five lobes, and the notches on each side of the tip of the leaf are U-shaped—U for sUgar—a good way to remember this. The leaves turn brilliant red and yellow in the fall—one of the most beautiful autumn sights.

Its sap is about two and a half per cent sugar. The Indians taught our early pioneers how to catch the sap, boil it, and make maple syrup or maple sugar. Forty-five to fifty gallons of sap will make a gallon of syrup. This tree is the main source of maple sugar and syrup even today.

The wood of the Sugar Maple is close-grained, pale in color, and valuable for all sorts of fine woodwork.

The Red Maple is a soft maple. Its twigs, flowers, seeds and long leaf stems are all red. Its three-lobed leaves turn a brilliant red in the fall. Its wood is used for furniture, charcoal, etc.

The Oaks have the family name of Quercus, given them by the Romans when they found the oaks in Britain early in English history. The name means "beautiful tree". And so it is. With the maples, the oaks are probably the best-known and loved of the broadleaved trees. It is not only beautiful, but one of the most useful as well. Its wood is used to make flooring, furniture, barrel staves, paneling, railroad ties, fuel and many other articles. Its acorns are enjoyed by squirrels, blue jays and other wild life. Pioneers made ink from the oak-leaf galls. Indians showed them how to grind the acorns between stones, making a sort of meal that, when cooked with water, was a mush that could be used for food.

The big family of oaks has two main divisions, the *White Oaks* and the *Red Oaks.* Each is easily identified by its leaves. If the oak

28

leaf has sharp points, quite needle-like, it belongs to the Red Oak family. If the lobes are more rounded, with no sharp tips, the leaf belongs to the White Oak family.

The White Oak has leaves that turn russet in the fall, and hang on the tree well through the winter. Its acorns mature in early fall. Squirrels often bury them for future winter use, forget to dig them up, and so a new oak tree sprouts. The acorns are a shiny brown, three-quarters to an inch long, and the shallow acorn cup comes up about a quarter of an inch. The acorns and their cups are attached to the limbs by very short stems. The tree may grow to be a hundred and fifty feet in height.

The California White Oak has leathery leaves with from seven to eleven lobes. Its acorns are about an inch long, and are very narrow. The cups are pale and warty, and grow up a third of the acorn's length. The acorns are borne singly or in pairs, and mature in one season.

The Bur Oak belongs to the white oak family. It can grow very tall, and has a beautiful, full spread. Its leaves turn yellow in the fall, and its early spring buds and leaves are also yellow. This yellow color, plus its unusual acorns serve to identify it.

Its acorns are very large, and they sit in high, mossy-looking cups that look almost like the nests of some tiny bird.

The Red Oak is a large, massive tree, not usually quite as tall as a White Oak. It has large acorns that sit in a very shallow cup, and grow very close to the limbs. The leaves are sharply lobed, with very sharp points. The wood is used for posts, floors, railroad ties and many other articles.

The Black Oak belongs to the red oak family, and is sometimes called the Yellow Oak because its inside bark is yellow. Its acorns grow in clusters close to the limbs, as with the red oak.

The Live Oak grows mostly in the deep south, around the Gulf area. It gets its name because its shiny green leaves stay on until they are pushed off by new leaves, so that the tree is always "live" looking. Its acorns are egg-shaped, shiny, chestnut-brown, about an inch long and a third of an inch wide. The acorn cup is a light, reddish brown, and its inside is lined with very fine hairs. The cup comes up about a quarter of an inch. The acorns are usually in a cluster of from three to five, and grow on short stems.

The Chestnut Oak varies from other oaks because its leaves are shaped like chestnut leaves, not like the usual, lobed oak leaves. They turn a light, very pretty brown in the fall. Its acorns mature in a year. They are a rich, deep brown, borne singly or in pairs, an inch to an inch and a half long, and almost an inch thick. A rough, thin, scaly cup covers them almost half their length.

The Osage Orange Tree is familiar to most mid-western children.

29

Early French explorers called it "Bois d'Arc", and used it, like the Indians, for making bows because its wood is flexible and straight-grained. Modern bows are still often made of this wood. It was first found in the territory of the Osage Indians, hence its name. The Indians used it to make a yellow and brown dye. Its sapwood makes a permanent yellow dye; the heartwood is brown.

This tree is used for hedges and windbreaks in open country. Its fruit, like rough, misshapen oranges, can be used in making holiday decorations.

The Redbud, like dogwood, is a small tree, native to some sections and widely planted in others for its decorative value. It has lovely, rosy flowers in spring, coming out before the leaves, so that the tree looks like a rosy mist. Its leaves are heart-shaped, and its fruit is in a small pod somewhat like a string bean.

Legend says that originally the tree had white flowers until Judas hanged himself on a redbud tree. Ever since, it has blushed red in shame. In some sections of the country it is called the Judas Tree.

The Sassafras Tree is one of the easiest to identify. Its leaves, twigs, bark, wood and roots all have a clear, aromatic smell and taste. Its roots, dried, can be steeped to make sassafras tea, considered to be a tonic by many people.

Its leaves, unlike most other trees, come in three different shapes on the same tree. They may be a simple oval leaf, a one-lobed leaf that looks just like a child's mitten, or a leaf with two lobes. It is sometimes called the Mitten Tree, because this leaf is easy to identify. The leaves turn yellow in the fall, then brown. The dark blue berries dangle on slender stems. Birds love them.

The sassafras can grow almost a hundred feet tall in mild climates, but stays a very small tree in cold ones. Usually where there is one sassafras tree, there will be a clump of them. It seems to like its own company.

The Sycamore is the largest broadleaved tree in North America. It can attain a height of a hundred and seventy-five feet, with massive girth. It is sometimes called the Buttonwood Tree because of the rough, button-shaped balls that hang singly on stems in the fall. The European plane tree has similar balls, but they hang in pairs, not singly.

The leaves of the sycamore are five-lobed, a bit like those of the hard maples, but the lobes are not so deep. They are yellow, then brown in the fall, shedding over a long period. The sycamore, like the birch, discards its old bark very visibly, and the mottled tree trunk is a good means of identification.

The Tulip Tree, sometimes called the Whitewood because of its soft, white wood, is one of our tallest broadleaved trees. It can grow two hundred feet in height, and its long, straight, pale grey, rough trunk gives it a very majestic look. In the spring it has yellowish-pink, tulip-shaped flowers about two inches in length but still fairly inconspicuous because they are usually so high up. When the petals fall they make a pretty color on the ground. The small open cones from the flowers can be seen on the tree after the leaves fall.

The leaves are quite large, leathery, and turn a beautiful shade of deep yellow in the fall. A tulip tree in autumn, against a blue October sky, is something to remember.

The Willows can be found almost everywhere where there is water. The bark is medicinal. The twigs are eaten by rabbits, deer, beaver and moose. The buds are enjoyed by many kinds of birds.

The Pussy Willow is usually a shrub-like tree growing along streams and roadways where its feet can keep wet. Its fat, grey buds give it its name.

The Weeping Willows are so familiar, with their drooping limbs, that they need no description. They are lovely in spring and fall. The stems are yellow against the winter skies.

The Black Willow is the largest of the willows, and is found along streams, lakes and swampy areas. It often grows in clusters of crooked trunks, very dark in color, and very picturesque. Its wood has almost no commercial value, but its bark produces tannin, used in tanning leather.

Palms are important trees found in the tropics all over the world. Some are native to, or have been cultivated, in the most southern parts of the United States.

The trunk of a palm tree is different from the trunks of other trees. It is made up of soft, spongy fibers within a thick sheath of very tough fibers that hold the tree erect. Water travels through these outer fibers. Palm leaves are called "fronds". A palm always keeps the same number of fronds. A new one rises from the top when an old one dies.

The palm has become a very symbolic tree. Its fronds were used in olden times to celebrate victories, and to crown the victors. In the Christian church, Palm Sunday, celebrating the triumphal entry of Christ into Jerusalem, is observed by the receiving of small pieces of palm fronds in the church. It is considered good luck to keep these bits until next year's Easter season.

The Coconut Palm is a "feather" palm. These are palms with fronds that have a strong midrib and small leaflets on each side. It was found growing in Florida by the early Spanish explorers. It probably came originally from Central America, since coconuts can float for long distances and are often carried by ocean currents. Inside a coconut is "milk" that can be drunk. Try it! It's good! The white meat that is just inside the coconut is called "copra". It is a food, and is used for making coconut oil. Copra is a valuable commodity in many parts of the world. The husks of the coconut burn easily. The trunk makes logs. The fronds make hut roofs, and the leaflets can be woven into mats and other useful articles. All these make the coconut palm a very useful and important tree in many lands.

The Royal Palm is another feather palm. It sheds its dead fronds, and so this tree looks neater and more slender than some of the others. Its trunk is smooth, white, and very graceful.

Date Palms, native to Arabia and North Africa, have been planted and grown successfully in southern California. The dates grow in cluster at the top. In their native lands, the date palms are an important source of food. Here they are mostly grown as ornamental trees.

Official State Trees

STATE	TREE	STATE	TREE
Alabama	Longleaf Pine	Montana	Ponderosa Pine
Alaska	—	Nebraska	American Elm
Arizona	Blue Paloverde	Nevada	Singleleaf Pinyon
Arkansas	Shortleaf Pine	New Hampshire	Paper Birch
California	Redwood		(White Birch)
Colorado	Blue Spruce	New Jersey	Northern Red Oak
Connecticut	White Oak	New Mexico	Pinyon (Nut Pine)
Delaware	American Holly	New York	Sugar Maple
Dist. of Columbia	—	North Carolina	—
Florida	Cabbage Palmetto	North Dakota	American Elm
Georgia	Live Oak	Ohio	Ohio Buckeye
Hawaii	—	Oklahoma	Eastern Red-bud
Idaho	Western White Pine	Oregon	Douglas-fir
Illinois	Bur Oak	Pennsylvania	Eastern Hemlock
Indiana	Tuliptree	Rhode Island	Red Maple
	(Yellow Poplar)	South Carolina	Cabbage Palmetto
Iowa	—	South Dakota	Black Hills Spruce
Kansas	Eastern Cottonwood	Tennessee	Tuliptree
Kentucky	Tuliptree		(Yellow Poplar)
	(Yellow Poplar)	Texas	Pecan
Louisiana	—	Utah	Blue Spruce
Maine	Eastern White Pine	Vermont	Sugar Maple
Maryland	White Oak	Virginia	Flowering Dogwood
Massachusetts	American Elm	Washington	Western Hemlock
Michigan	—	West Virginia	Sugar Maple
Minnesota	Red Pine	Wisconsin	Sugar Maple
Mississippi	Southern Magnolia	Wyoming	Balsam Poplar
Missouri	Flowering Dogwood		(Cottonwood)

Something To Make

The craft projects that follow are all relatively simple. Any of them can be modified or adapted to suit the individual skills of the adult and child, and to the types of natural materials available locally.

These projects depend largely upon "tree trimmings" for the natural materials used. Substitutions can be made if such "trimmings" are not native to the area.

Look for such natural materials in the nearby woods, parks, playgrounds, streets, yards and shopping centers. Explore the local area. The adventure of finding, collecting and identifying is part of the larger adventure of shared conversations—questions, discussions, and shared information, followed by the fun of creating something out of nature's "tree trimmings".

How Old Was That Tree?

Make a *stump rubbing* and figure out the approximate age. Try to find a stump that was cut fairly smoothly and recently. Then take a long strip of narrow, white paper (the kind used in adding machines is perfect). Stretch the paper across the smoothest diameter of the tree trunk as taut as possible. Tuck the edges over and thumbtack them to the bark on either side, so as to hold the paper securely in place.

Then hold a soft lead pencil, a piece of charcoal, or a colored marking pencil almost parallel with the trunk surface, and rub it at right angles to the annual rings. Work from the outer edge to the center. The two halves may not come out exactly alike, but they will serve as a check on each other.

The wider the annual ring, the more rainfall that year. Very narrow rings will indicate very dry years.

What was going on in the nation when that tree was very young? Look it up in the history book and find out.

Pinecone Packets

A wonderful Thanksgiving or Christmas gift to anyone with a wood-burning fireplace. Collect a bushel basketful of pinecones— any variety. Divide them into two piles. Buy a pound of copper sulfate from the hardware or drugstore and a half pound of boric acid from the drugstore. Mix the copper sulphate into a gallon of water, and the boric acid into another gallon of water, in separate buckets.

Put the pinecones—as many as will go—into mesh bags like those used to hold onions and oranges. Tie the tops of the bags. Immerse each bag into one or the other of the two solutions, and let stand for several days. Then take out the bags, empty them onto pads of newspapers, and let dry thoroughly. Use tongs or sticks to remove the bags, and keep the hands out of the solutions.

When the cones are thoroughly dry, pack some of each into net,

33

cellophane, or plastic see-through bags, tie with bright ribbon, add a sprig of green—and presto! A very pretty gift that will burn with beautiful green and blue flames.

Try treating corncobs the same way. Let them dry out before putting them into the solutions, and then let them dry thoroughly before packing into gift packages.

Pinecone Pin

Glue five "petals", or pinecone scales, into the cup of an acorn. Glue a seed or bead into the center so that a pretty flower shape is formed. Add a bit of moss if it will look pretty. Attach a stem made of a green or brown pipe cleaner. Glue several "petals" to the stem for leaves. Spray or paint with plastic spray or lacquer.

Or, omit the stem, and glue a bit of felt to the under side of the acorn cup. Insert a small safety pin.

Woodsy Earrings

Glue a tiny bit of dry moss and a few pretty seeds into a nice design onto a small bit of smooth bark. Spray with plastic spray or lacquer. Glue earring "findings" to the back of the bark. Wear the earrings with outdoor clothes.

Try putting the seeds into a tiny flower design, or arrange them to look like eggs in a tiny nest.

Pinecone Pete

An open pinecone turned upside down makes his body. Attach a brown pipecleaner up near the top for his arms. Insert other pipe-cleaners near the bottom to form Pete's legs. His feet are large lima beans, sprout end at the front. His head is an acorn on a pipe-cleaner neck. A circle of felt with a small hole in the center and fitted over the acorn will make a floppy hat. Pete's arms can hold a cane, or flag, or skis—or a placename card.

Pinecone Pete

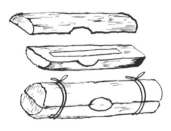

Twig Whistle

34

Acorn Pendant

So easy! So pretty! Nice to wear with sweaters. Pick out an acorn and cup that is just the right size and shape. Gently separate the cup from the acorn, then with a bit of Elmer's or Sobo glue, put the cup back on. This is to make sure that the acorn and cup stay together, because they usually separate when they dry out.

Then very carefully insert a small brass screweye into the bottom of the cup. The pendant will hang from the screweye, cup on top. Add a coat of shellac for gloss and preservation. When the pendant is perfectly dry, hang it on a thin chain, or narrow bit of leather thong, or a length of strong yarn. (A narrow leather shoelace makes a good thong. Measure and make long enough to go over the head.)

Twig Whistle

Find and cut a tree twig about three inches long and a half inch to an inch thick. Slice the twig in half lengthwise. Hollow out a small section of each half, about in the middle. Scoop out a small area for the mouth to blow into along one side of each half so that when the twig is put together again these areas will be joined. Place a blade of grass in the scooped out section of one side. Put the other side back in place, and tie the two ends together with a bit of string, good and tight. Then blow hard into the scooped out section—and it will make a fine squawk.

Pinecone Jewelry

Like eucalyptus pods, pinecones can be cut or sawed into beautiful rosettes and other shapes. Strip the cone first, very carefully, so as not to break it. A hacksaw does the best job of cutting a pinecone straight across into fairly thin rosettes, or diagonally, or in slices, all of which make interesting shapes. Drill holes where necessary if the finished piece will be used for a necklace, or strung for any reason. Sandpaper the piece carefully until nice and smooth. Then lacquer or varnish it for gloss and permanence. Mount on a thong for necklace or pendant, or glue to pieces of felt, then add a small safety pin if piece will be used as a pin.

Wooden Belt or Necklace

When a tree is pruned, save a branch that is from three-quarters of an inch to an inch and a half in diameter. Saw it across into coin-like pieces that are about a quarter of an inch thick or slightly thicker, depending upon how you like it. Drill two or four holes in each piece. Sand them until smooth, then shellac. When dry, run a leather or nylon thong through the holes. Use the number of pieces needed for the size of the belt or necklace. A narrow leather shoelace makes a good thong for a necklace. Knot it between the wooden

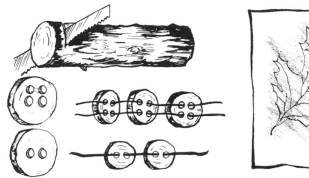

RED OAK

Wooden Belt or Necklace   Leaf Rubbing

rounds if desired. Knots will help hold them in place and will look nice. Narrow lengths will make an interesting bracelet.

These rounds also make very attractive buttons for sweaters or sport jackets.

Wooden Pendant

Similar to the wooden belt or necklace. Saw a round from a tree branch two to four inches in diameter. Carve it into an interesting free-form shape if desired. Drill a hole for a thong, cord or chain. Sandpaper until beautifully smooth, then shellac. Hang around the neck and wear with pride.

Select the wood for its color. Cedar will give a lively red pendant; holly a white. Apple wood will be very light. Walnut will be brown.

Eucalyptus Pod Jewelry

These pods vary among the varieties of eucalyptus, but all of them are interesting and attractive. They make very pretty jewelry when dried and painted gay colors. Explore ways of using the pods. Cut them open, cross-cut, or slice them diagonally. Use a needle and thread to string the pods; dental floss is fine, or nylon cord can be used.

Try gluing small, pretty stones inside a pod. Add shells, or odd-shaped wood, or other natural materials. Make the necklace long enough to go over the head so that no clasp will be needed. Or make into bracelets or earrings.

Pinpoint Telescope

This project doesn't use native materials, but it makes observations in the outdoors a bit clearer—pinpoints them, as it were. Find a

36

mailing tube about an inch and a half in diameter, and cut it into a length of about five to six inches. Cut a disk of cardboard just big enough to fit into the tube. Make a smooth, neat hole in the center of this disk. A thumb-tack will make a good hole. Tape or glue the disk into the tube about a half-inch from one end. Make sure that no light comes in around the disk.

Look through the other end. This telescope will not magnify, of course, but it does aid the naked eye by blocking out all the surrounding details when it is focused on one object, such as a pinecone on a branch, or a tulip tree flower, or the like.

Leaf Rubbings

One of the nicest ways to decorate notepaper, paper napkins, table mats, book covers or other articles made of paper. Very easy, too.

Find and bring back several leaves with different and interesting shapes. For notepaper, use a sheet of writing paper folded once, or into quarters. Place the leaf between one fold, vein side up. Then rub a crayon across the paper on top, going in one direction only. The outline of the leaf will appear. Then write the name of the tree from which the leaf came—and the pretty sheet of decorated notepaper is ready to use.

These rubbings, if cut out carefully and mounted on construction paper, or cardboard, will make a pretty border for a bulletin board, or for the wall of a room. They will form a ready reference to answer "What kind of tree did this leaf come from?"

Christmas Decorations

Christmas and other holiday decorations are easy and fun to make out of natural materials. Many are attractive in their own woodland colors. Others may be sprayed to suit any decor. The following suggestions can be modified, and other natural materials sustituted for those not native to or available in the local area.

Pinecone Elf. An attractive, gay little ornament for the Christmas tree or mantel. or for use on placecards at the Christmas or other holiday table. Its decorations may be varied to suit the occasion.

Glue a wooden bead, spool or other roundish article to the top of a pinecone. It will be the elf's head. Paint simple little features on it with ink or crayon. Add a cone-shaped cap of red cloth or paper. Trim the bottom petals of the pinecone so that the elf will stand alone, or attach a string to the cone, so that the elf may be hung. Spray the cone any color, including white, gold, or silver, if desired. The elf will be attractive if left natural, however.

Sycamore Ball Ornaments. The balls from the sycamore tree, and the balls from the sweet gum and European plane tree make

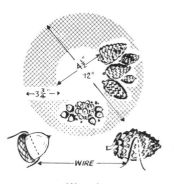

Pinecone Elf   Wreath

very attractive hanging ornaments for the Christmas tree or decorations to be placed in a wreath or swag. Cut them off from the tree, leaving the stem attached if possible. If pulled, the stem will break off. Spray them any color, attach a string to the stems, and hang on the tree. To add additional color, attach some red rose haws to the ball by pushing a pin through the haw and into the ball.

Tumbleweed Ornaments. Southwesterners use these prickly plants for holiday decorations. They can be fitted together by their prickles into almost any shape. Often they are piled into a cone shape suggesting a Christmas tree, then sprayed white, silver or gold and decorated with glitter. Here are several ideas.

Trim small ones into circular shape, attach a string for hanging. Spray with white, gold, silver or other color. Dust with glitter if desired. Hang on a Christmas tree, in a window or doorway, or other place. They will look very gay and airy.

Make wreaths by pressing several small, trimmed tumbleweeds together into the shape of a wreath. Decorate as above. Use for doorways or table decor. A candle placed in the middle of a table wreath looks very pretty.

Combine larger tumbleweeds into a cone-shaped Christmas tree for table. Decorate as above.

Use for other holidays or special occasions. Spray to suit the color scheme. Combine into other holiday shapes.

Better use gloves when trimming or working with tumbleweeds. They are *very* prickly.

Hemlock Cone Tinsel. The tiny little cones of the hemlock tree are too small to show very well when used singly, but just try stringing them! They make lovely "tinsel" when sprayed white, red, gold, silver, or other color. Easy to make by assembling a number of the little cones, stringing or tying them to a string, painting or dipping

38

them into the color to be used. Allow them to dry, then drape them over the limbs of the tree. Or gather a dozen or so into a ball, paint, and hang as ornaments. Scatter glitter over the cones for added sparkle.

Kissing Balls. Stick sprigs of pine or other evergreens into a styrofoam ball. Decorate with red ribbon, leaving a length of the ribbon to hang from the bottom of the ball. Attach a pretty spray of mistletoe to this ribbon. Hang the kissing ball in a doorway, just high enough to miss touching the heads of those passing through. Anyone caught under the mistletoe must give—or claim—a kiss.

Christmas Wreaths. Wreaths may be made from a wide variety of natural materials. Use the ones native to the area, and follow the general directions for the traditional evergreen wreath suggested by the Office of Community Recreation Services of New Hampshire.

Assemble a supply of the natural materials to be used, plus a supply of #30 galvanized wire from the local dime or hardware store. Double wire frames are available from local florist shops, or use one-quarter inch hardware cloth (heavy wire screening). Cut a 12-inch circle of the hardware cloth with tin snips or heavy shears. Then cut a four and one-half inch circle out of the middle, leaving a flat frame three and three-quarters inches wide.

Choose the sprays or pieces to be fitted into the wreath, and wire each piece in place by looping the center of each piece with the wire. Pass the ends of the wire through the frame, twist the ends tightly together, and clip them one-half inch from the frame. Bend these ends back against the frame.

Fill in any gaps with smaller sprays or other items. To wire nuts and acorns, drill a small hole near the base and thread the wire through it. Keep adding sprays and other items until the wreath is full and rich in appearance.

Plan a special point of interest for the wreath. It might be a cluster of nuts, or sprays of holly or mistletoe, or a cluster of Christmas tree balls, or palm fronds, or real or artificial fruit. Use an uneven number of any such additions. They always look better, for some reason, than an even number.

Keep adding material until the wreath frame is completely covered and you are satisfied with its appearance. Attach a hook for hanging, or hang it by a long ribbon or silk cord.

If desired, spray the wreath front and back with plastic or satin-finish varnish. It will bring out the natural colors and make the wreath more durable. To protect the wall or door behind the wreath, cut a circle of cardboard and a circle of felt the same size. Glue the felt to the cardboard, then wire the cardboard to the back of the frame.

Follow the same general procedures when making a swag for door or wall.

Felt-Tincan Printing

Select any tree leaves with well-defined shapes, and use them as patterns on pieces of felt. Glue the felt cut-outs onto the sides of a can, leaving an inch or so of margin top and bottom for use in holding the can roller. Pour a thin layer of poster paint into a shallow pan, such as a cookie tin or foil container. Roll the can over the paint, then, holding it at the ends, roll the can over a large sheet of paper until it is covered with an overall leaf design. Use for mats, for bulletin board decorations, book covers, or other decorations.

Smudge Prints

Nice and messy! Select a well-shaped leaf, and lay it on a sheet of paper. Wrap the index finger with a small square of soft cloth (cheesecloth is good), holding it on the finger with a rubber band. Dip the cloth-covered finger into a few drops of food coloring, ink, or paint. Holding the leaf in place with the left hand, smudge color by stroking the cloth-covered finger across the edges of the leaf onto the paper until a complete outline has been made. Lift the leaf carefully—and a pretty leaf silhouette will show up. Use the paper for leaf identification, for mat, bookcover, or other decorative use.

Carbon Paper Prints

A good way to get clear prints for a leaf print collection. Place a full-grown leaf, vein side down, on the carbon side of a piece of carbon paper which has been placed on a pad of newspapers. Put a sheet of newspaper over it and press for several minutes with an iron set for pressing wool.

Then remove the top newspaper and the leaf. Place the leaf carefully on the sheet of paper to be printed, cover with another sheet of newspaper and press as before. When the newspaper and leaf are removed, the leaf print will show up very clearly, and the print can be labeled for identification.

Foil Prints

One of the very easiest. The results can be mounted or laminated into very decorative mats or other paper articles.

Place a large leaf, vein side up, on a pad of newspapers. Cover the leaf with heavy duty aluminum foil. Then press hard but carefully all over the leaf with the hand, until the outlines of the edges, veins and stem of the leaf show up clearly. Cut out the outline carefully and mount it with cellophane tape, or laminate it (and others) between mat-size sheets of wax paper or cellophane. Press the edge with a warm iron to hold permanently in place.

Spatter Prints

These make beautiful designs for mats, for framing, and for other decorative uses. Use the same procedures to spatter print grasses and small flowers. Two general methods can be used.

Place the leaf, or leaves and grasses, into a pleasing design on a piece of construction or other type of paper. Pin the material into place, using straight pins stuck in upright so that they will not throw a shadow when sprayed. Then, holding a spray can of acrylic, water color, poster paint or ink, spray carefully so that the outlines of the materials will show but the paper won't be covered with the paint. Stand well away from the sheet of paper when spraying so as not to over-spray. Let dry first, or remove the leaf with great care so as not to smudge. When dry, mount the print for framing. Dark paper and light paint will make an interesting print. So will light blue paint on a darker blue paper. Work out other pleasing color combinations.

The older method of spatter printing is still a very good one, and children enjoy it. Place the material to be printed as above. Then hold a piece of 3- by 5-inch window screening in the left hand, about six inches above the paper. Dip a small, stiff brush (an old toothbrush is fine) into a small amount of paint or ink, rub the brush over the screening, so that the paper is full of small spatters. Continue until the material is outlined, and the spatters are in a pleasing design. Then lift the material carefully, or let the print dry first. When the paper is dry, mount the print as above. Label it if identification is wanted.

Magic Autumn Leaves

Fun to do, and a pleasant way to learn and use colors. Cover a large piece of paper with different autumn colors, rubbing them heavily into any sort of design, anywhere on the paper. Use shades of yellow, orange, green, brown, red, etc. Then, when the sheet is completely covered, rub over all those lovely colors with a coating of black crayon.

Take a nail file, blunt scissors, or other tool that won't tear the paper, and draw free-hand leaf designs on the paper (outline real leaves if desired). Once the leaf outline shows through to the color, scrape off the rest of the black in that area—and out shines a pretty, fall-colored leaf! Continue until the sheet of paper is full of leaf designs, or until a pleasing design is formed against the black background.

Laminated Wax Paper Mats or Screens

An easy way to dress up a table or window, or to decorate in other ways. Collect a number of leaves with pretty colors and shapes, remove their stems, and press between newspapers under a weight until dry. Then arrange them into a pleasing design on a sheet of wax paper cut the size of a table mat, or to fit into a window. Remember that a plate will cover the middle of a table mat, so that a design there will be wasted. When satisfied with the design, cover that sheet of paper with another piece of wax paper. A paper clip along the sides may help to keep the two sheets exactly together. Then press with a warm iron until the waxed papers stick to each other, making one thickness. Scallop the edges if desired.

Use this same method for making designs of grasses, flower petals, flat seeds, ferns, and other natural materials.

Table or Window Transparencies

Very similar to the laminated wax paper mats, but more permanent —and expensive! Arrange the pressed, dried leaves, grasses, flowers or other flat natural materials between sheets of self-adhesive paper. "Contac" is one brand name.

Each mat will require a piece of transparent, self-adhesive paper twelve by eighteen inches, and one piece of patterned or colored self-adhesive paper the same size. Peel the paper backing from the colored or patterned sheet, and place the nature materials on it in a pleasing design. (Better work out the design first, because once the material is laid on the sticky surface it is almost impossible to remove or change it.)

Once the design is in place, peel off the backing from the transparent sheet. Hold the ends with the finger tips, one end in each hand, sticky side down. Let the sheet bend in the center, so that the center of the top sheet and the edges are in line with those of the bottom sheet. Lower the top sheet carefully until the centers touch. Then allow each end to roll into place. Smooth firmly with the fingertips, stroking from the center out, until the two sheets are sealed together. If air bubbles are caught, let the small ones stay in. Prick any large one with a pin to let the air escape, then smooth over the tiny hole. If the edges aren't exact, trim the mat—or start over with a new one! These mats are quite permanent, and may be cleaned by wiping with a damp cloth or sponge.

For a transparent see-through effect, use two sheets of the transparent paper. Very delicate and pretty designs may be made by using ferns, grasses, and small flowers. This project has to be done with care, but the results are very rewarding.

Angel Feathers

These are skeletonized leaves, easy to make and attractive to use. They may be mounted on fine, florist wire for use in dry bouquets and flower arrangements, and mounted or laminated to make dramatic and decorative prints, mats, lampshades or other decorative articles.

Select the leaves to be used, including several types for contrast and interest. Boil these for a half hour in a quart of water, in a granite or porcelain pan, in a solution of one quart of water and one teaspoon of baking soda. Let the solution cool, then spread the leaves out flat on a pad of absorbent paper (newspaper will do, but the newsprint may smudge the leaves).

Scrape the leaves very carefully with the blunt side of a knife until all the fleshy parts of the leaves are removed. Put the skeletons into a solution of two tablespoons of household bleach and a quart of water, and let them stay there until they look white. Then rinse, place the "angel feathers" between sheets of paper toweling and press under a weight for twenty-four hours. When thoroughly dried and pressed, these skeleton leaves are very lacy and attractive. Use thin florist wire if the stems are too short for a flower arrangement. Or use the skeleton leaves in making laminated mats or transparencies.

Owl Family Shadowbox

A delightful decoration or gift. The frame shadowbox can be made from any box the right size, minus the top, and placed on its side, so that the bottom of the box becomes the back of the shadowbox. Paint or cover the sides and back of the shadowbox, using a color that will show off its contents.

The base of the little scene can be a mussel shell, a piece of bark, or a blob of plaster of paris. It must be large enough and heavy enough to hold the finished scene upright. Glue or cement it to the bottom of the box.

The fence on which the owl family sits is made with two small twigs for the fence posts, and two smaller but longer twigs for the fence rails. The posts must be cemented onto the base of mussel shell, or glued into holes dug into the bark or plaster of paris. The rails should be glued about one-quarter inch apart, and one-quarter inch below the tops of the posts. Be patient. Let the frame dry into place so that it will stand securely.

Mother Owl has a hemlock or larch cone for a body. Her head is another cone trimmed to a smaller size. Use the clippings to make tiny ears on the top of her head, and other bits for her feet, all glued to the cone, then to the rail.

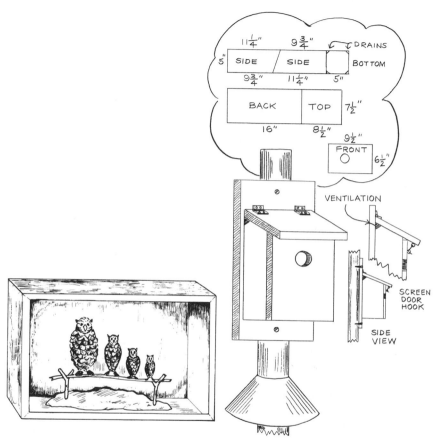

Owl Family Shadowbox

Bluebird House

Baby Owls are three hulls of buckwheat or other small seeds or pods. Trimmed "petals" from a hemlock cone may be used. Add tiny bits of dried grass stems for their tiny ears.

Glue or cement the shell, bark, or plaster base securely to the base of the shadowbox. Cover the front of the box with clear cellophane or plastic wrap. Result—an endearing little scene. But work slowly and carefully. It takes patience, but is worth it.

For the Birds

Craft projects that not only use natural materials, but also provide food, water and shelter for birds help to expand interest from the world of plant life into the world of birdlife. Make them, and use them to lure birds into closer view for more enjoyment.

Bird Baths. Sink an old hubcap, or top from a garbage can, into the ground so that the rim is even with the ground. Place rocks around the rim for a rustic look. Keep it filled with water. Small birds will use it for baths and for drinking.

Dig out any size area at a spot in the yard fairly close to a tree or shrub, so that birds will have a safe place to perch while drying off. A circle or oval about two or three feet in diameter makes a good pool. Slant the hole so that it will be shallow around the rim, deeper in the center, but not more than four inches deep. Then line the hole with ready-mixed cement according to directions on the bag. Cover it with a wet cloth or piece of plastic and let the cement "set" for several days until it is thoroughly dry. Then plant around the edges, or decorate with pretty stones or shells, if desired. Fill it with water, and watch the birds use it.

Provide a large pan with low sides, and fill it with very fine sand. Many birds love to take *dust* baths, so the sand will have to be replaced as it gets pushed out. Place the pan in a sunny, but sheltered, spot near a tree or shrub if possible so that a cat won't surprise a bird. If the setting is sufficiently rural, you may even see partridges come up for a dust bath.

Bird Houses. Birds are fussy about their nesting places. The bluebird-house plan shown here comes from the Office of Community Recreation Service of New Hanpshire. It is a good, basic plan. Adapt the dimensions for other birds, using the list given later, and write to the National Audubon Society for additional information if desired. Adapt the material for the box to fit whatever is available in the home workshop. Scraps of wood, plywood, shingles, wood from crates and boxes can all be used.

The baffle at the bottom of the sketch is added to protect the nest from marauding cats or squirrels. It may be omitted if not needed.

The size of the entrance hole, its height from the bottom, and the height of the birdhouse from the ground are all very important. Some houses might include a perch at the entrance. Bluebirds do not need a perch, and omitting a perch will discourage sparrows and starlings that might try to move in. The hinged roof makes the box easy to clean after the nesting season, and thus makes the house more permanent.

For this bluebird house, the entrance hole is one and one-half inches in diameter, and is six and three-quarters inches from the bottom of the box. The house should be from four to ten feet above the ground. Weathered wood is best, but the house may be painted or stained a dark brown or green by using thinned paint and wiping off the excess. The box should be put up by April first, at the latest.

Bird House Dimensions

Bird	Interior size Inches	Depth Inches	Hole diameter Inches	Height above floor Inches	Ht from Ground Feet
Bluebird	4 x 5	8½	1½	6¾	4–10
Wren	4 x 5	6–10	1	5–9	6–16
Phoebe	6 x 6	6–10	Open front	Open front	8–12
Robin	6 x 8	8	Open front	Open front	6–12
Titmouse	4 x 4	8–10	1⅜	6–9	6–15
Nuthatch	4 x 4	7–10	1¼	6–8	10–20
Chickadee	3¾ x 4	8–10	1⅛	6	6–12
Flicker	7 x 7	15–18	3½	12–16	6–20

The National Audubon Society has all sorts of birdhouse information. See RESOURCES.

Bird Feeders. Nothing brings birds closer for observation than providing them with safe places to eat, and keeping the food supply replenished. Place the feeders in the open so that birds can see any enemy approach. Here are several varieties that are easy to make.

The net bags in which onions, oranges and other commodities are packed make excellent *suet feeders.* Fill them, tie them securely, and hang them from the limb of a tree or from a clothesline. They can be nailed to a tree, too, if squirrels, cats and raccoons are not a problem. Such feeders are very popular with a wide variety of birds, including woodpeckers, nuthatches, chickadees, orioles, jays, grackles and many others.

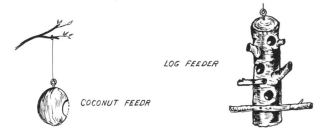

LOG FEEDER

COCONUT FEEDR

Bird Feeders

Another suet feeder can be improvised by nailing a wire soapdish to a shingle or small strip of wood, and then nailing that to a tree trunk. Keep the soapdish filled with suet. The shingle or wood strip keeps the suet from injuring the bark of the tree.

A small log—white birch is pretty—makes a good feeder. Bore a number of large holes in it, nail several pieces of wood to it for perches, and then fill the holes with a mixture of peanut butter, melted suet and seeds. Hang from a strong screweye with wire at the top—and watch the birds come to it. The chickadee is likely to be the first to venture to any new feeder. Keep the holes filled.

46

A *coconut* makes an attractive and useful feeder for small birds. Saw off one side, and scrape out the meat (use it for some good dessert!). Fill the cavity with a mixture of peanut butter, melted fat or suet, and seeds. Hang from a strong screweye at the top. Use strong wire because it will be fairly heavy.

The *pinecone feeder* is one of the easiest and prettiest, and small birds love it. The cone, to be very effective, must be a large one— the longleaf pinecone is excellent. Wind a length of wire securely around the top of the cone to hang it from a limb. Stuff the spaces between the "petals" with the suet-peanut butter-seed mixture. When the cone gets wet, it will close its petals. As it dries out, they will open. It makes quite a barometer!

Seed feeders can be improvised from wooden boxes. Take off two sides of the box, nail an inch-high strip across the open sides at the base to prevent seeds from blowing out, and then keep feed in it. Birdseed may be bought in many supermarkets, feed and hardware stores. A less expensive way is to buy sunflower seed separately, and mix it with chick feed, much less expensive than the wildbird mixtures, and the birds don't seem to know the difference!

Cheeseboxes—the ones that the big rounds of cheese come in— make good seed feeders. Drill holes around the edges for four wires which can be brought up together and twisted around the limb of a tree.

Magnifying Glass

Another project that helps with other projects, even though it is not strictly a nature craft project.

Find a little piece of window glass, and put a drop of salad oil on it. Then hold the glass about an inch above the object which will then be magnified several times. Place the object on a sheet of white paper for best results. Look at tiny things such as the barbs on a feather, a fish scale, or a small insect.

PART II

Crafts From
Nature's Gone-To-Seeds

Something To Look For

The grasses, weeds and shrubs that grow in the fields and along the roadsides often have interesting seeds, seedpods, burs, and berries. Note where they grow—check their soil, the water nearby, the amount of sun they need.

Look to see what eats the seeds. Which birds eat what? Look for small animals that hide among the plants. Try to get a look at a white-footed mouse, a raccoon, an opossum, squirrels, rabbits. Look for the many butterflies, bees, ants, beetles, caterpillars, dragonflies, fireflies. Listen to the crickets and cicadas. They are all well-camouflaged, but they are very likely *there* for those who really look.

Collect and look at all the seeds that can be found. Notice their shapes, colors, sizes. Look for seeds that parachute away, seeds that whirl down like little helicopters, seeds that stick to anything that comes near, seeds that are so pointed that they can get into the ground easily.

Look at the designs made by the leaves and the seed heads of grasses and weeds. Look at the soft colors of the dying foliage.

Look for the tree fruits the acorns, pinecones, beechnuts, hickory nuts, persimmons, crabapples, walnuts, pecans. Crack them open and really *look* at the designs inside.

Look for animal tracks in sand, mud or snow. Look near the bases of trees for squirrel tracks. Look for the tracks of a raccoon in the mud near a pond or stream. It will resemble a small, human foot with extra long toes. The opossum's track will look just like a small human hand, complete with thumb. Look for the V-shaped tracks of birds, too.

Watch the flights of birds. Which ones soar with very little wing movements? Which fly in pretty dips? Watch a humming bird hover, and perhaps fly backwards.

Look for an ant hill. Watch one ant as it goes foraging. Follow it on its trek. See if you can find a hornet's nest—but keep away unless it is an old, deserted one. Look for mud-daubers' nests, those queer little lumps of clay put up against the sides of a barn or other building.

Look at the wonderful colors and designs on beetles. Even the harmful ones are beautiful. Try to copy the designs on paper with crayons.

Look for, collect, and dry some of the grasses, seeds, burs, nuts and flowerheads. They will be fun to use in craft projects. Look for the seedpods of poppies, iris, columbine. Look for the big pods and seeds of lilacs, sweet pepper bush, locust trees, bittersweet. These are useful project materials, too.

Something To Talk About

Grasses

We take grasses for granted—but how could we ever live without them? We make our breads out of grasses—wheat, oats, barley, rye, rice. The animals we raise for food must have grasses. How could cows, beef cattle and sheep live without grasses? Grasses cover the earth, and without them life on our earth would likely perish.

In the fields and along the roadsides, look for different kinds of grasses. Gather and dry them, and use them for making prints (see PART I) and other craft projects. Look for some of these very well-known grasses:

Old Witch grass, sometimes called Tickle Grass. Just get a bit of it stuck inside your sock or pants leg, and you will see why. It has large panicles that spread out somewhat like a feather duster. In the fall it gets very stiff and brittle, and it can blow around like a small tumbleweed.

Yellow Foxtail grass seeds came into this country with the early settlers, as stowaways in their clover and grain seed. It grows from one to four feet tall, matures early, and has spikes or "foxtails" from two to four inches high.

Sand Bur has burs about a quarter of an inch in diameter, stiff, sharp, and strong enough to go through shoe leather!

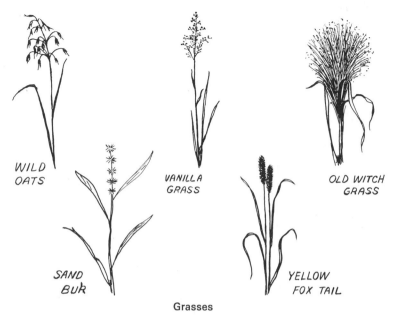

WILD
OATS

VANILLA
GRASS

OLD WITCH
GRASS

SAND
BUR

YELLOW
FOX TAIL

Grasses

Vanilla grass smells like vanilla when it is dry. In olden days it was strewn in churches so that the congregation would walk over it, and the smell could perfume the church.

Wild Oats is very graceful with its hanging spikelets. It grows from two to four feet tall. The hulls are covered with stiff, brown hairs.

In the fields and along the roadsides, along with grasses, you are likely to find two herbs and several very interesting weeds.

Tansy has foliage that looks like parsley. It has yellow flowers, and its leaves are very aromatic.

Yarrow is sometimes called Thousand Leaf because the leaves are so finely toothed, and very ferny looking. The flowers are white and flat-topped. This plant is also very aromatic.

Legend says that Achilles used yarrow to cure the wounds of his soldiers at the siege of Troy. For that reason, its scientific name is Achillea.

Teasel was brought to this country to supply weavers with its burs which were used to tease up the nap of cloth. The burs were also used by women to card wool so that it could be spun into thread and then woven into cloth. Now it is just a weed with an interesting, rough, thimble-like seed container on top. It is often used in dry plant arrangements.

Baneberry has a strange-looking fruit. The white variety is often called Doll's Eyes because they *look* just like dolls' eyes, complete with a black pupil. It belongs to the buttercup family.

Pokeweed is a plant that is all red and green. It has dark green leaves, dark purple-red fruits, and very red juice in its stems. Children used to use it to make red ink. Its seeds and roots are poisonous if eaten by humans, but birds love them.

Roadsiders

Besides the grasses, wildflowers, weeds, and many interesting shrubs grow along roads and in fields. Some of them furnish important food for the birds.

Pokeberry Bush has dark purple berries that the Indians—and children—once used for war paint.

Wild Cherry has pretty white blossoms in the spring, and sprays of dark red berries in the fall. Over a hundred varieties of birds enjoy these berries. It belongs to the rose family—note its five-petaled flowers.

Two things make this shrubby tree unpopular. When it is cut, its withered leaves are poisonous to horses and cows. The tent caterpillar uses it frequently for its big net-like "tents".

Shadbush, or Shadblow is so named because it blossoms when the shad used to come up the rivers to spawn in the spring. Today many of the streams that once swarmed with shad are so polluted that they can no longer support any fish life.

In the West, a species of the shadblow is called Service Berry. It has small, rosy, apple-shaped fruits, much prized by birds.

Red Elderberry has dark purple berries that children use for dyeing their skin, and mothers use for making jams and jellies—unless the birds get there first!

Bittersweet grows as a shrub or vine. One of its names is Waxwork, descriptive of its orange-red fruit in the form of a pod that splits into three parts, showing the orange-red berry inside. Its flowers are white and inconspicuous. Bittersweet is so prized as an autumn decoration that it is becoming very scarce.

Nature's Orchestras

Talk about the hum of the bee or mosquito. This hum is made by the vibration of the wings. The short-horned grasshopper makes a rasping sound by rubbing its hind legs against the front wing cones. The long-horned grasshopper, katydid, and cricket make a noise by rubbing the underside of one front wing over the upper side of the other. The rib that runs across the underside of the front wings has a series of teeth like a file. The upper side of the front wings has a rough surface. When the wings are rubbed together, they make a high note, like a whirring sound. Listen for it in a sunny field or meadow.

Katydids make their "Katy *did*, Katy *didn't*" sounds at night, in the same way. They are fairly large, green insects, and are hard to see because they are so well camouflaged.

The chirping cricket makes its chirp in the same way.

Woodboring beetles make tapping or ticking sounds. The sound is made by the head of the insect striking the wood while it burrows.

To Pick or Not to Pick

A good, general rule for picking wildflowers is in a rhyme:

> Pick if you must one flower face,
> If nine more blooms are left in place;
> Two feet square must hold that many,
> Otherwise look—but don't pick any.

In many states it is against the law to pick some of the rare wildflowers, trees, shrubs and ferns. Trailing arbutus, trillium, gentian, dogwood, mountain laurel, and rhododendron are on many state conservation lists. Find out, and talk about, what flowers and plants should *never* be picked in your state by writing to your state conservation department in the state capitol.

Talk about private property. *All* land belongs to somebody—a person, a group, a town, county, state, or the federal government.

Talk about good outdoor manners: Not going on private property without the owner's permission; never leaving gates open, or breaking fences; never walking or running through planted fields, lawns and gardens; never carving or cutting trees, uprooting flowers or disturbing boundary markers.

Two plants belong definitely on the Hands Off list—the poisonous poison ivy, and poison sumac. Poison ivy has very tempting red leaves in the fall, but its leaves, stems, roots—even its smoke when burned—are poisonous, and can cause itchy white blisters to appear on the skin. "Leaves three, let it be" is a good warning.

Poison sumac is equally virulent, but is not so prevalent since it prefers swampy ground. The berries of this sumac are *white*, whereas the berries of the non-poisonous variety are dark red and stand up in a spire. It is called the Staghorn Sumac. "Berries white, dread the sight; berries red, have no dread".

Flight

Clouds fly across the sky. So do sand and dust. So do seeds and spores (see PART III). So does pollen from plants. Look for the "flowers" of evergreen trees in the spring, and see how the pollen gets blown, so that new seeds can develop. Look for the pollen hanging on many of the grasses. Most grasses are wind-pollenated.

Some seeds go into flight by parachutes, like dandelions and milkweed seeds. Look for the seeds of elms, maples, ash, and ailanthus trees. They have tiny wings that whirl them down and away like little helicopters.

Some animals are good gliders. The flying squirrel, sometimes seen at feeding stations at night, has flaps of skin attached to the front and hind legs and a flattened tail that acts as a rudder. Some fish, such as the sailfish and the swordfish, can leap up into the air and glide back because their large fins keep them right side up and let them glide down headfirst.

Insects are flyers. So are butterflies and bats. Some butterflies, such as the monarch, actually migrate great distances every year.

Birds are what we think of first as flyers. Some have big, long wings for lifting and gliding. Some have small wings that must work constantly to keep the bird aloft. Watch the birds, and observe their flight patterns. Notice how their feathers overlap so they can control air currents that touch them.

Really *look* at a feather. Notice the long, hollow shaft that is filled with air. Notice the barbs, like little zippers, that keep the web of the feather locked together so that air won't pass through it.

Why is flight important? It is used by birds to get food, or to escape from enemies. It is used in migration. It is used by plants to assure new growth. In other words, flight is necessary for survival.

Something To Make

Some of the gone-to-seeds, such as acorns, have been mentioned in PART I, but the smaller seeds, burs, pods, nuts, berries and the like are also good craft material. Many of these can only be found and collected in the late summer and the fall, but others can be found in winter and spring.

Some of the projects here are included to help a child become more familiar with the flying insects that are also part of the world of nature, often unnoticed because of their size or camouflage.

Craft projects that involve looking and touching can be just-for-funs. Every project doesn't have to be useful, or result in some beautiful object, although some projects will. Discovering that seeds come in a fascinating array of sizes, shapes, colors and textures is as important as making something out of seeds. Really *looking* at burs and pods before making a Bur Rabbit or a Milkweed Angel is the most important step in the project. An appreciation of the small, wonderful, often unseen world of nature's treasures is more important than any craft use of those treasures.

Leaf-and-Flower Crown

Children love these, and will enjoy collecting a supply of pretty leaves and flowers to use in making them. Leaves with long stems work out best. Cut or tear off the stems, keeping them separately. They will be the pins for the wreath. Try using colored leaves in the fall. Pretty!

Overlap two leaves, bottom side up, and with the fingernail or a pointed stick, tear two small slits through the two leaves where they overlap. Push a stem "pin" through one pair of slits and up through the others, thus pinning the leaves together. Continue until the wreath is large enough to fit the head, or to go over the head to form a neck wreath.

Then turn the wreath over and decorate it with some flowers—daisies, black-eyed susans, asters, violets, or other flowers in season can be used. The stems of the flowers can be stuck under the stem "pins". Very pretty!

Leaf People

Collect a number of different kinds of leaves in various shapes, sizes and colors. Press them between paper toweling, under a weight, until they are dry. Then paste each to a card or sheet of paper. The leaf makes the *body* for the Leaf People. Add crayoned or painted heads, arms, legs, hands, and feet to make funny and pretty Leaf People in all sorts of poses.

Bur Bee

A Bur Bee is just a bunch of cockleburs or other large, thorny burs, modeled together into a bee shape. Add twigs and leaf stems for feet and antenna.

Bur Rabbit

Bur Rabbit is like Bur Bee. Model his body out of a handful of burs. Add leaf ears and twig whiskers. If possible, collect some milkweed "silk". Remove the seeds, and stick the milkweed silk into the burs for the rabbit's fur. Try making Bur Birds the same way. Or make Bur Baskets—very pretty when filled with moss and small woods-pretties. Just model the burs into a basket shape, and make a bur handle, or attach a twig or grass handle.

Nut Bur Rabbit

An open beechnut bur makes the body. Add a bit of modeling clay flattened into a triangle for the bunny's head. Circles of white poster paint make the eyes, set in the sides of the head. Add a dot of black for the pupils.

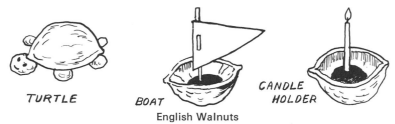

TURTLE   BOAT   CANDLE HOLDER

English Walnuts

Add beechnut hulls for ears, glued to the sides of the modeling clay.

Balloon Bug

A real just-for-fun. First find and observe a real, live caterpillar. Notice its stripes, or polka dots, and other color designs on its body. Make a sketch of that design in crayons.

Blow up a long balloon. Cover it with strips of paper toweling dipped into wallpaper paste. Put on three or four layers of this sticky paper, then let it dry out. It may take several days to get thoroughly dry, but be patient. When it is dry, paint the balloon bug with the design of the real caterpillar. Add pipecleaner legs and antennae. You'll have a Giant Caterpillar.

English Walnut Novelties

These split so nicely that they make all sorts of interesting projects. They can be made into little fortune holders, or tiny-gift holders by hollowing out the shells, putting the fortune paper or gift inside, rescaling the shells with glue or masking tape, and painting them. (See MAKING CHILDREN'S PARTIES CLICK, Stackpole 1967.)

Make a *Walnut Boat*. Wrap a paper triangle around a matchstick for a mast and sail. Stick the mast into the shell by adding a bit of modeling clay at the bottom of the boat. Sail it in the bathtub or dishpan.

Make a *Walnut Turtle* by pushing a marshmallow into a shell-half. Pinch out pieces of the marshmallow so that the head, the feet, and tail overlap the shell. Turn the shell over, and there's a partially edible turtle.

Pick out shells that will sit nicely. Put a bit of modeling clay in the bottom of the shell. Insert a tiny candle, and then use the little *Walnut Candleholders* for a special occasion. Or use the empty shells to hold a few mints at each place setting.

Make a *Walnut Mouse*. Take a hollow walnut shell-half, put it down on a piece of cardboard, and outline it with a pencil. Then cut out the outline. It will be the bottom of the mouse.

Select a marble that is slightly bigger in diameter than the shell is deep. Into the cardboard cut a hole *slightly* smaller than the marble, but smooth and big enough for the marble to move within it. Tie or glue a five-inch bit of string to the cardboard for the mouse's tail.

Glue the cardboard to the shell with the marble inside. Cut mouse ears out of paper and glue them to the shell. Draw the mouse's eyes and whiskers, or glue on whiskers made of broom straws. Then place the walnut mouse on an inclined plane—and watch it roll down.

Insect Apartment

Remove the lid from a cigar box. Decorate the inside of the box, and prop up some twigs inside it for the insects' furniture. Cut a hole in one end of the box. Slip the box into an old nylon stocking. Knot the stocking at the toe end, and pull the knot up close to the uncut end. Stuff the open end of the stocking into a cardboard tube inserted into the hole cut in the box. The tube becomes the "door" for putting insects into the box, and for giving them tiny bits of food.

Another *Insect Motel* can be made by cutting windows in pint-size containers. Cover one window with cellophane or plastic wrap. Cover the other window with a bit of wire screening, taping it into place with masking tape or adhesive tape. Put a small ball of moist cotton inside. Add a bit of dog biscuit for food—not very much. Then introduce the tourists.

Try to find two crickets, a male and a female. The male will have *two* prongs in the rear. Then listen to the male cricket put on his concert. Or bring in several fireflies, and watch them glow on and off—but let all the tourists leave in the morning.

Cricket Cage

Easy to make and fun to use. Place a glass lamp chimney in a flower pot filled with moist soil, or make a plaster base for the lamp chimney, filling it with an inch or so of moist soil. Put in a pair of crickets and feed them almost anything—a bit of apple, lettuce, bread, dog biscuit—but just a tiny bit. Put in something for the crickets to hide in and under. A bit of crumpled-up dampened paper towel will do nicely. Cover the glass lamp chimney with a bit of cheesecloth or wire screening so the crickets can't jump out.

Then watch the crickets and see how the male cricket makes his chirp. The life span of the male cricket is about a month.

The cricket makes a good thermometer, too. Count the number of chirps in fourteen seconds and add forty. The result will be pretty close to the temperature of the weather.

Feather Bird

A project that keeps going on for some time. The youngsters try to find and bring back any feather they can find, after any trip, walk or hike. Draw the outline of a big bird on a piece of cardboard, cut it out, and place it against a door or wall. Every time a feather is found, that feather is glued to the bird, wing feathers to the wings, tail feathers to the tail, down to the throat, etc. In time, the bird will be completely feathered—and a very strange bird indeed.

Bird Nest Garden

Find a discarded nest and bring it home. Plant it in a flowerpot, with soil below, around and over it. Keep the soil moist. Very likely *something* will sprout from some seed used by the bird for food, or brought in with the nesting material.

Milkweed Pod Decoration

These long pods lend themselves to all sorts of interesting craft projects. They make the winged angels for the Christmas tree, and can be gilded and sprinkled with glitter for extra shine. They also make *framings* for little natural scenes, and these, too, make pretty tree ornaments.

To make one of these framings, spray the outside of the pod gold, and paint the inside of the pod a sky-blue. Glue a bit of short grass or moss to the bottom end of the pod. Then glue a tiny figure of an animal, or a bird—a tiny gull looks very pretty—inside the pod, as part of the little scene. A loop of string can be run through a hole punched into the top of the pod, or glued to the pod with a bit of masking tape.

An *Angel* for the Christmas tree can be made by combining a milkweed pod and the dried head of Queen Anne's Lace—it looks

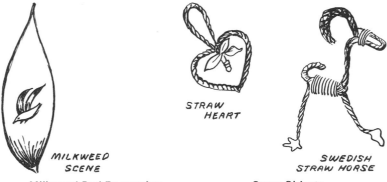

MILKWEED SCENE

STRAW HEART

SWEDISH STRAW HORSE

Milkweed Pod Decoration   Straw Objects

like a dry bird's nest. The angel's wings are the milkweed pods. Glue them to the flowerhead, and spray lightly with white or gold paint. Very airy and lacy!

Miniature Plaque

First comes the fun of looking for, and finding, pretty little natural objects. Perhaps some tiny hemlock cones, an acorn cup, a pretty, small, gone-to-seed grass, a small seedpod, a bur, milkweed silk— anything small, pretty and dainty. When a good supply, to provide plenty of choices, has been collected, give it time to dry out thoroughly. Hang any weeds or flowerheads upside down for drying.

Then make a pretty frame. A coffee can lid is a good size for these miniature plaques. Glue a loop of string on the back, or attach it with masking tape, so that the plaque may be hung. Spray the lid with gold paint.

Then get out the collection of miniatures, and select some of them to make a pretty, graceful design inside the frame. When the design is just right, very carefully put a bit of glue on each piece, and glue it into place. When the glue has dried thoroughly, you can give your design a touch or two of gold paint to bring it out. Use a fine brush for this, because varying degrees of the gold is prettier than just covering everything with the paint. These plaques are very pretty when several are hung together in a group. They make nice little gifts, too.

Straw Objects

The straw that the Swedes use in so many delightful straw crafts is a special variety not grown in the United States. Salt hay, used as a mulch in gardens, can be used as a substitute. So can dried grass stems, and strips of corn husks. All of these substitutes can be braided, adding extra pieces as one length gets used up, until the necessary length is made. To keep these braids fairly smooth, tie them every few inches with a bit of red string. It will not only hold them securely, but also look gay.

When the braid is finished, bend and tie it into whatever shapes you like. Bent into a small circle, it will make a pretty, pale wreath for the Christmas tree. Bent into a heart-shape, and tied with red ribbon, it can be a Valentine, or a tree ornament.

A *Straw Goat* can be made by using two braids. One is bent to make the legs and middle part of the body. The other braid makes the tail, part of the middle body, neck, head and horn. The two middle sections are bound together with red yarn. The head is made by looping the braid and binding it with yarn. Corn husks can be tied together, too, to form body, legs, head and horns of goats or horses.

58

These straw, grass, or corn husk creatures all make very interesting Christmas decorations, bringing a Swedish touch to the American decor.

Corn Husk Dolls

A lovely pioneer craft project that today's children will enjoy just as much as yesterday's.

Take the husks (shucks) from green corn and dry them out for a few days, or use ripened husks. Dampen the husks in a bucket of water while working with them. It will make them more flexible, and less likely to break or split. Save the corn silk for making the hair for the dolls.

For *little* dolls, use one husk. Cut it about four inches long and fold it. Tie a string or bit of yarn about a half-inch from the top to form the doll's head. Arms are cut two inches long, and put between the folded husk. Tie the ends of the arms to make hands. Tie a piece of string or yarn to make the waist. That's all for a girl doll. For a boy doll, divide the lower part of the husk to form legs. Tie at the ends to make the feet.

For *larger dolls*—and they are prettier and more interesting—use the full length of the husk. Tie several together to form a head. Turn this knotted top inside out so that the knot is inside, and the head is puffed out a bit. Tie to form the neck. Use husks to form the arms. Braid them and tie at the two ends for wrists. Put the braid through the body husks and tie at the waist. For boy dolls, divide the legs below the waist, and braid the legs. Tie at the ankles.

These dolls may be dressed to represent Indians or pioneers. Paint the eyes, nose and mouth with softened crayons, or rub a bit of lipstick for mouth and cheeks, a bit of eye shadow for the eyes.

Cornstalk Fife

Cut a piece of cornstalk about ten inches long and one and a half inches in diameter. Run a stiff wire up it to remove the pith. Close one end of the cornstalk with paraffin. Burn or bore a hole near the closed end, and burn or bore two more holes near the open end. Blow into the hole near the closed end, and by using the fingers on the other two holes, three musical notes can be played.

Nature Notepaper

This is one of the very nicest craft projects, but it will take time and care. It is too involved for the very young child, who can, however, help collect the necessary supplies, and select some for the designs. Older children will be very proud of themselves when they see the results of this project. Half the fun of it, however, is in looking for, finding, and collecting a wide variety of natural material for drying and then for use in making the designs on this lovely, parchment-like paper.

Collect a supply of small, graceful flowers, leaves, vines, tendrils, grasses and ferns. Small, delicate-looking objects will work out better than larger, coarser ones. Press all of them carefully between paper toweling, weighted down by books, or piles of magazines. Keep similar supplies separate from each other for easier choosing. Cardboard boxes, where they can be spread out, make good containers.

Make a pattern for the size of notepaper you want, to match the size of the envelopes you plan to use. OR—buy boxes of inexpensive, single-fold notepaper with envelopes. Use this notepaper for the writing paper, and the paper you make for the outside cover for it. In other words, the bought paper will be the filler, the made paper, the decoration.

The next instructions are for single sheets, but it is a good idea to work on a large table, or the floor, and make a number of sheets at the same time.

Put a piece of wax paper over the paper pattern you made. Let the wax paper be slightly larger. On the wax paper place one or more pieces of the natural material in a pleasing design. Keep it simple and airy. Delicate designs look prettier.

Place a *single ply* of facial tissue over the design with care. With a soft brush—a pastry brush will work out well—wet the tissue thoroughly with a mixture of half water, half Elmer's (or other) glue. (Prepare a supply of this in advance.) Press any air bubbles from the center of the tissue to the outside edges. Sprinkle on a bit of glitter or a few sequins if you like, but they are not at all necessary. Leave the wet sheet out flat to dry overnight.

Next day, press the sheet between pieces of brown wrapping paper at "Rayon" heat, wax-paper-side up. This pressing with a hot iron melts the wax, holds the design in place, and makes the paper take on a parchment look.

Place the wax-paper-design sheet on the pattern. With the metal edge of a ruler held tight against it, tear the paper to size, giving a handmade look to it. The parchment paper will now be the same size as the pattern, and will fit the envelopes.

This parchment paper can be used as is, or, as noted above, can be used as a cover for plain notepaper. The parchment paper can be used for other purposes, too, such as mats, lampshades, bookcovers.

When prepared with care, and when designs are well-planned, this paper is very pretty indeed. A box of ten sheets of it makes a fine gift, or a popular item for sale at a bazaar.

PART III

Crafts From
Nature's Hide-Aways

Something To Look For

These will be the hard-to-sees, the be-quiet-and-listen, the under-logs, the in-trees—all the little hide-aways in woods, fields and gardens. They are the easy-to-pass-bys, but for those who take the trouble and time to look for them they are nature's pretties. Some fly among the tree-tops. Some race across tree limbs. Some run along the ground, or under the ground. Some grow on rocks, some on dead logs, some in marshes, some among dead leaves.

The woods and fields are full of sounds as well as sights. Listen for the hum of bees and other insects, the rustle of a chipmunk in the dead leaves, the scolding of a squirrel, the song of a bird. Stand still, keep quiet and try to hear all of them.

Look down and see the little fiddleheads of ferns, or tiny flower blossoms almost hidden in the leaves. Look at the small, trailing plants that once were giant trees—the Club Moss, the Ground Pine, the Trailing Cedar.

Look for the little sweet-smellers—the Trailing Arbutus, the Pipsissewa, the Shin-leaf, Chimaphila, and Rattlesnake Plantain with its striped leaves. Look for the Pink Ladyslipper, with its moccasin shape and long shoelaces; Hepaticas with their heart-shaped leaves and blue, white, pink and lavender flowers; Wild Ginger, with its leathery leaves and dark red blossoms like bells, hidden under the leaf mold.

61

Look at the blossoms of *trees*. Many people never notice any of these except the fruit trees, but all trees have flowers, sometimes very small and hard to see.

Look at the shades of color in mosses; the many sizes, shapes and shades of coloring in mushrooms; the small, white flowers and later on the red berries of Wintergreen and Partridge Berry, both such pretty little woods-trailers. Feel the soft wool that is wrapped around the new fiddleheads of ferns.

Look for beetles or other bugs under a piece of loose bark on a tree. Lift up a dead log and see what is under it—then put the log back in place. Look for loose dirt that may show where a woodchuck has been digging his burrow. Look for the big piles of leaves high up in the trees. They are the squirrels' summer homes.

Look for bits of moss on dead wood; a mushroom to bring back to use in making a print of its spores; tiny creatures like crickets, fireflies, beetles and caterpillars that may be kept in an insect cage for a day or so, and then released.

It takes *time* to find and to see the hide-aways. They are easily passed by on a hike or in a car. Stroll slowly. Stoop. Lean down— and LOOK.

Something To Talk About

The hide-aways always come as *discoveries*. It is an adventure to find them. It is exciting to suddenly come upon a pink ladyslipper, see a squirrel in the act of hiding a nut in the ground, hear the tapping of a woodpecker high in a tree, taste a leaf of wintergreen, come upon a red mushroom in the green world of the woods. These hidden treasures are the "Look what I found!"—almost invisible to those who hurry, or who don't really look.

Finding them is good training in observation. Enjoying them is the best possible training in appreciation. Talking about them is the way to share the wonder. This in turn will lead to curiosity about them, and an interest in learning *more*. Talk about:

Wildflowers

Many of the prettiest wildflowers are woodsy plants, blooming in the spring. Look for the way that the very early Skunk Cabbage seems to spurt up through the still-hard ground in March. April and May will bring in the fragrant Trailing Arbutus with its leathery leaves, and its small, waxen pink or white flowers. It usually grows in patches, and sometimes it can be smelled before it is seen. Hepaticas are blue, white, pink or lavender, and their slender stems grow out of a cluster of lobed leaves, shaped like a liver— their name *means* liver. Dogtooth Violets grow in patches, too.

Their leaves, with their distinctive stripes, help to identify them. Some people call this flower "Adder's Tongue".

The name of the Pipsissewa is Indian. Its roots spread underground, and its flower stems hold up very fragrant, waxy, white flowers. Shin-leaf also sends out underground roots, and has bell-shaped, white, fragrant flowers. The pink ladyslipper is one of the prettiest and most common of wild orchids, but it is getting quite rare. It grows in woods where there are evergreens, and a patch of them in the woods is a sight to remember. Solomon's Seal has little bells blooming up its graceful, long stem. False Solomon's Seal carries all its flowers at the very end of the stem. Both are woodland flowers. Marsh Marigolds are like clumps of gold standing in water as they bloom in early spring. Wild Azalea, sometimes called Wild Honeysuckle, grows on low, lacy bushes. The flowers are pink and white, and look very airy. A golden variety grows wild in the Southern Highlands of the United States, called Flame Azalea.

Wild Geranium is a pretty pink or lavender. Its leaves look just like the geraniums of pots and windowboxes. Mountain Laurel is sometimes sold in florists' shops, but is much lovelier in its natural setting. Its buds are twisted like small, pink shells in a cluster.

Talk about conservation. Find out which flowers and plants are on the special conservation list in your state. Then LOOK, don't pick those flowers.

Never try to transplant a wildflower or plant unless you can reproduce the place where it grew wild. This usually is impossible, because wildflowers, especially woodland flowers, require deep or dappled shade, moisture, leaf mold, and the protection of other wild plants around them. Most of them, when transplanted, seldom live more than one season, if that.

Every section of the country has its own native wildflowers. Write to your state department of conservation, and to the extension service of your state university, and ask for their publications on the wildflowers and plants or your region. Then see how many of them you can find. Learn their names, and where they grow. You'll soon have a most interesting hobby.

Ferns

Look for some of them in moist places, along streams, in ravines, at the base of rocks, in wet meadows. Look for others along roadsides, and in fields and meadows. Ferns are fascinating plants without flowers or seeds, but producing spores.

Many legends exist about ferns. One tale says that ferns bloom with small, blue flowers on Midsummer's Eve, and that anyone who catches their seed at midnight will have magic powers.

Another legend says that a pinch of fern seed in the shoes will make a person invisible. Another legend says that a pinch of fern seed in the shoe will give the wearer the power to locate lost articles. The tellers of such tales were perfectly safe because ferns don't *have* seeds!

Talk about how old ferns are as plants. They once, millions of years ago, grew fifty feet tall. Fern fossils are sometimes found in coal, looking just as they look today, only much, much larger.

Talk about the funny, coiled-up fiddleheads. Look for them in April and May. Touch them. Feel how soft they are, in their wooly or silky covering.

Cinnamon Fern is one of the very first to come up in the spring. Its fiddleheads are covered with what looks like white wool.

Christmas Fern fiddleheads lean over backwards, and are covered with what looks like silk. Their tips stay curled up even after the leaflets on the stems open out. This fern stays green all winter.

Bracken grows almost everywhere in the world except in deserts. Its fiddleheads' tips stay curled up like the claws of an eagle, even after the fronds have grown out. Bracken can grow fifteen feet tall. It is called Brake in some lands. Legend says that bracken gives people protection against goblins and witches, and that burning bracken will bring rain.

Deer Fern and *Sword Fern* grow in the western states, and like christmas fern, stay green all winter.

Maiden Hair Fern is one of the very prettiest of the ferns. Its midrib is circular or semi-circular, giving its delicate, lacy fronds a very airy look. Its jet black stems are a good distinguishing mark.

Mosses

Talk about the mosses, one of the oldest forms of plant life, even though they seldom grow more than six inches tall. They grow all over the world, in cold and hot climates, but not in deserts, because they must have water. There are more than twenty-thousand kinds of mosses! They live all year round. In time of drought, they just stop growing, sometimes getting very dry and crisp, but with a good rain they come back to their soft texture very quickly, because they are very absorbent.

Take a simple moss leaf, put it in a saucer of water, and it will produce little green threads in a few days. Then tiny buds will appear on the threads, each capable of producing a new plant.

The *Hairy Cap Moss* is one of the easiest to find. Look for its little stems that look like a tiny sprig of cedar, and the stems that bear the little hairy cap, which is a spore case.

Pincushion Moss is another that is easy to find and to identify. Sometimes its "pincushions" grow two or three feet across. It is a

64

pretty pale green when damp, and becomes grey and crumbly when dry.

Lichens

Lichens are found all over the earth, and some scientists wonder if they are not to be found on some of the other planets as well. They are a very primitive form of plant life. They have no stems, no roots, and no leaves, but they manage to exist, and even eventually eat into rock.

Litmus paper is made from lichens. In ancient times people learned that lichens could yield a dye that had the strange quality of turning red when touched by an acid, and blue, when touched by an alkali.

British Soldiers is one of the prettiest of the lichens. Look for it on rotten wood in shady woods. The knobby little spore cap is bright red, just the color of the uniforms of the Redcoats.

Pixie Cups are like their name—little cup-shaped fungus just big enough to please an elf.

Horsetails

Once upon a time, millions of years ago, horsetails were enormous trees in the coal age forest. Now they grow only a few feet tall in sandy, gravelly soil, often along country roads. Look at the stems, joined like pipes. Pick one and see how the joint pops when separated from the stem.

Ground Pine, Trailing Cedar and Shining Club Moss

These forest trailers that form a mat across the ground were once tall trees in the coal age. Get down at eye level with them. They still *look* like trees. You will feel as though you are in a miniature forest.

Mushrooms

Talk about them. What IS a mushroom? The main part of a mushroom is out of sight, in the ground. It is a mass of white, thread-like branches. The part that is above the ground is really the fruiting part that bears the spores. It is first a tiny little blob just below the surface. This grows into a button shape, then to a dumbbell shape, and then finally to the cap-and-stem shape that we are used to seeing. They grow *very* fast. Some can grow up in a single day. That is why one day we see them, the next day we don't. Their caps look like little umbrellas in many species. The ribs of the umbrella are called "gills", and can be different colors.

Talk about the millions of spores in the gill, and make a mushroom print of these spores (see Mushroom Printing in this Part).

Some spores are white. In other species, they may be black, pink, brown, rust or yellow.

Talk about the little *Brownie Cap,* looking just like a tiny coolie hat. Look for *Glistening Ink Caps,* with their shiny scales.

Look for and talk about a *Fairy Ring,* that mysterious circle of mushrooms that pop out in meadows, golf courses and other smooth areas. They grow in that ring shape because those white, underground branches spread always outward as the centers die. Legend says that these rings show where fairy gold is buried, and that fairies dance within that circle on moonlight nights.

Talk about *poisonous* mushrooms, and warn the child never to eat wild mushrooms unless they have been picked by an expert.

Many of the poisonous mushrooms have a ring around the stems and a flattened *cup* at the base (the cup of death).

Birds

Make a Bird Caller (described in this Part), and use it to lure birds into closer view. But dress inconspicuously, move quietly, and don't make any noise by talking or whispering. You will probably see some of these familiar birds:

Blue Jays will scream "Thief! Thief!" and tell all the woods that you are coming. Jays don't migrate in the fall. They build their nests of sticks, lined with rootlets, up in trees. The eggs are greenish, with brown speckles. Jays have been known to eat the eggs and young of other birds, and they often monopolize a feeding station. They are very intelligent birds, and it is said that they can be taught to talk. Even though they are greedy and noisy, they bring color and interest to the woods and gardens.

Nuthatch. When you see a grey bird coming down a tree headfirst, it is very likely a nuthatch, sometimes called "the upside down bird". They have strong feet and sharp beaks. They hide food under loose pieces of bark—and sometimes forget where, so that other birds find it and eat it. Their nests are holes in the trees. The eggs are speckled white. Nuthatches stay all winter, and are frequent feeders at the feeding stations. They are very fond of suet.

Chickadees also stay all winter, and are friendly little birds, easily tamed to eat from the hand. They are small and fluffy, and their cheerful "Chick-a-dee-dee-dee" is easy to identify. In the spring this song changes to a long-drawn-out "Pho-e-b-e". Don't confuse it with the rapid "Phoebe! Phoebe!" that announces the Phoebe in the spring.

Juncos, in their dark grey uniform with white bibs, look like tiny nuns. They love winter, and a flock of them is said to prophecy a snowstorm. They look for shelter in ravines, and under bushes and evergreens, and they prefer to eat on the ground rather than at a feeding station. Their nests are on the ground, well-hidden. The eggs are bluish-white, marked with reddish-brown.

Woodpeckers also stay all winter, and are frequent visitors at the suet box. The Downy Woodpecker and the Hairy Woodpecker are just alike, except the Hairy is at least twice as big. The males of both species have a red blaze across the back of the head; the females are just black and white, no red.

Woodpeckers have very strong, stumpy tails that they use as props against a tree-trunk when they are searching for food within the bark. Their beaks are very strong and pointed, for they are very good borers. The nests are in holes that they bore in trees. The male and female take turns boring the hole. The eggs are laid on the chips of wood that they have bored off. The babies are born naked and blind.

Animals

Woodlands have all sorts of interesting animal life, but it is hard to see it. Animals are shy and wary, but certain familiar ones can often be found.

Rabbits. Everyone knows Peter Rabbit of the Cottontail family. Look at a wild or tame rabbit, and see how strong those hind legs are. Notice how the rabbit raises its little white tail up over its back when it runs, like a little flag.

Mother rabbit digs a hole in the ground six or seven inches deep. She lines it with soft straw and weeds, then with down from her chest and sides. This nest is called a "form" because she shapes it to the form of her body. She gives birth to from six to eight babies, and she keeps them well covered with straw and weeds. They are perfect little miniatures of their parents, and can leave the nest in about three weeks.

Look at a rabbit when it is sitting up to eat. Notice how the eyes are set in the sides of the head, so that the rabbit sees only out of one of them in one direction. Watch how fast they can run. They can make thirty-three miles an hour.

Woodchucks, called "Groundhogs" in some places, belong to the squirrel family—note those four long front teeth. They live in "burrows". Groundhogs dig lots of holes to provide different entrances and exits. These are often under large rocks, tree roots, or stone walls.

They hibernate in the fall, when the weather gets cold, and come out in the spring. Groundhog Day is February 2, and legend says that if the groundhog sees his shadow on that day, he will return to his burrow—and we will have six more weeks of winter.

Chipmunks are pretty little animals about nine inches long, with long white stripes down their chestnut-colored bodies. They have cheek pouches in which they can collect food and take it down into their winter quarters for storage. The chipmunk can fill those pouches so full that it looks as though it had mumps.

They dig holes deep in the ground, often under rocks or tree roots, and they line their living quarters with grasses to make them soft and warm. They also provide themselves with extra rooms for the storage of seeds, nuts, dried berries and other food so that they will not go hungry in the winter. They live, half asleep, very comfortably all winter underground. Chipmunks can be tamed very easily.

Moles live mostly underground and are therefore almost blind. They have very strong, shovel-shaped front feet for digging their "runs" that they use for roads and for hunting their food. They eat earthworms, cutworms and other grubs, digging their tunnels and going hunting mostly at night or early morning. Their tunnels may look bad on a smooth lawn, but the moles eat many very destructive grubs.

Squirrels, either red or grey (in Westchester County, New York, there is a variety of *black* squirrels, and in Olney, Illinois, a variety of *white* ones) are great tree planters. They hide acorns and other nuts in the ground, for future winter use, and then forget to return for them. Squirrels have their claws set in such a way that they can come down a tree headfirst—something no cat can do. They live in hollow trees, and construct large "treehouses" of leaves in the treetops for summer homes. Look for them high up in the trees.

Turtles. In the spring, often after a rain, turtles come up out of their winter holes, and the females go looking for a place to lay their eggs. They hunt for a sunny place in a field or meadow, scoop out a shallow hole with their flippers, and lay several eggs that look very fragile, but which really have very tough shells. Then the turtle replaces the soil and lets the sun do the rest!

Turtles eat berries, slugs, worms, and early mushrooms. They have a remarkably long life span. They can retract their heads, legs and tails so well that their shell acts like a coat of armor in case of attack by some other animal. They hibernate below the frost level in the winter.

Something To Make

Nature's hide-aways are sometimes so fragile and delicate that they should be looked at but left alone. Some of the plants are too rare to pick. Some, like some of the more prevalent ferns, can be picked sparingly for use in craft projects, such as making prints and mats (see Part I).

The projects here are all relatively simple, although some will take a bit of time and patience. The best thing about the hide-aways, however, is the *finding* of them—learning to be observant enough to see the tiny hidden things so easily passed by.

Sometimes looking at them with a strong magnifying glass will show new wonders of color, texture and design.

Size is not too important in nature. A mushroom may be small, but its life force is so strong that it can push up through an asphalt driveway. Nor does beauty go only to the largest. Some of the most beautiful things in nature are the little hide-aways.

So admire them, look for them, talk about them, learn more about them. *Then* a craft project will be a really exciting and educational experience.

Acorn People

Collect acorns of different sizes and shapes, with and without the acorn cups. Paint or carve faces on the acorns. Use one acorn cup for a cap or hat, and another acorn cup for a stand. Dig out a small hole in the cup to be used for the stand, put a dab of glue in it, and

Acorn People

set the acorn head in it securely. Glue the cap on, too. Make an Acorn Person to put at everybody's place at the dinner table, or set them up in a row for an exhibition.

Add other decorations to the heads as you think of them. A tiny feather for an Indian head, yellow yarn hair for a Dutch girl, a tall paper hat for a witch.

Acorn Miniatures

Children love tiny things. They have a very special fascination. Acorns make delightful miniatures.

The acorn cups make charming little saucers. Cut the acorns in two and hollow-out each half, being careful not to break the shells of the acorns. Presto! Tiny little soup bowls on little dishes for a doll's dinner set.

Cut the top off an acorn, dig out a hole in the side, insert a straight twig or stick—and there's a very realistic little pipe that any boy doll would like to have.

Moss Stand

Very simple but interesting. Find a small piece of dried wood, or driftwood, or root, interesting in shape, and flat enough to sit steadily on a table. Scoop or scrape out a fairly shallow depression somewhere on it. Fill this little bowl-shaped area with a bit of moss. Just a drop or two of water once in a while will keep the moss green, and it will bring a bit of the woods into the living room. It also can be used with a pretty flower arrangement.

Moss Scene

Take a good look, from a ridge or hillside, at the fields in view below. Note how they vary in color, shape and size like a patchwork quilt. Then look for moss of different textures and colors, and collect small pieces of each. Bring them back carefully, so as not to crumble or mix them.

Select a dish with sloping sides. Put a shallow layer of sand in it for drainage, then a layer of soil—wood soil if possible. Place the pieces of moss in a field-like arrangement, and see how pretty it will look in the same sort of patchwork-quilt sort of way. Keep the moss moist, and the field scene will last indefinitely. Add a tiny evergreen, or a twig tree, or miniature figures of animals or people. Sometimes they will add extra interest to the "view".

Twig Dolls

Use the veins of leaves, or their stems, for pins. Dress little twigs up in leaf or flower dresses. Add acorn caps, if you like.

Bark Masks

If you live where there are trees that shed their bark in long, big strips, collect some. They make wonderful masks, sometimes very weird and outlandish. You can add a bit of paint, or glue on grasses or other natural materials to make them look even more horrible. Hang them along the walls of a fence or patio.

Eucalyptus bark with its mottled colors is very effective. So is birchbark, and the rough bark from the shagbark hickory. Just remember not to pull bark from a living tree unless the bark has been pushed off and is already dead.

Come-To-Life Garden

In the early spring, before plant growth starts, dig up a three-inch square of top soil from the woods or garden, and put it in a flat flowerpot or other container, such as a foil pan, or an unused terrarium. Provide drainage by putting pebbles and sand in the bottom. Water well, cover the top with a piece of glass or cellophane, and place in the light. Then watch to see what will come out of the mystery garden. Very likely there will be both plants and insects!

Hidden Leaf and Flower Life

In very early spring, while trees and bushes are still dormant, cut some short branches from different kinds of trees. Stick them into moist sand, or into a vase of water—and watch the tight little leaf or flower buds swell, burst out of their winter coats, and become leaves or flowers.

Cut branches of forsythia and place them in water. In a week or two leaves and yellow flowers will open on those dead-looking branches. Branches of fruit trees will do the same.

Miniature Models

Making tiny models of the home site, street or playground is a craft project that will encourage observation as well as imagination.

Collect twigs, bark, grasses, burs, seedpods, pebbles and other natural materials. Then, using bits of string or wire, construct lawns, houses, tents, tepees, chairs, docks, boats, stockades, corrals —whatever comes to mind. Use them for a miniature pioneer village, an Indian village, a modern street scene.

Villages, houses, and other dwellings need people and animals. Make twig people and twig animals, including both wild and domestic animals.

Try to be reasonably authentic. Use books to check costumes, types of tepees or cabins, which wild animals lived there. Use the layouts for storytelling, to act out, or to illustrate some favorite story.

Bottle Gardens

This will take patience, but the results will bring pleasure to all who see it. Find a wide-mouthed glass bottle with a screw top. Place it on its side. Glue corks or bottle tops to one side, so that the bottle will lie on that side without rolling.

Then put in a small layer of coarse sand for drainage, then a layer of garden soil. Make this soil layer a bit uneven in depth, so that it won't look totally flat. Add a pretty rock for interest, and to change the eye level. Then moisten the soil very carefully so that it won't spatter up on the sides of the bottle. Use a fine sprayer or atomizer if you can find one.

Then comes the hardest—and most interesting—part of the project. Collect bits of moss, tiny trailing plants, perhaps a miniature evergreen seedling. Add a few seeds—grass seed will come up fast. Plant all these things in the soil by using sticks, long-nosed tweezers, long-handled spoons or anything else that will help to push the little plants into place and cover their roots with soil.

Punch some holes in the screw-top lid for ventilation, then screw it onto the bottle. Keep this woodsy garden out of the direct sun. If too much moisture forms in the bottle, take off the screw top for an hour or two. If the soil seems to dry out at all, spray it again, lightly.

A fishbowl, brandy glass, goblet or old aquarium will also make very handsome woodsy gardens. These are all called "terrariums". They will require a piece of glass over the top to conserve moisture. They make wonderful Christmas gifts because they bring a bit of the outdoors into the indoors, when it is cold and bare outside.

Toy Gardens

Similar to terrareums, but not so permanent. These are really small "arrangements", nice for gifts, and especially nice for breakfast or sick-a-bed table.

An aluminum foil pie or cake tin makes a good container. Give it a thick layer of sand. In the sand stick pebbles, shells, twigs, small flowers or other materials. And add a tiny butterfly or bee made out of paper or cellophane and attached to a toothpick or thin wire so that it will hover over the garden. If the flowers or other natural materials are living, keep the sand moist. If the toy garden uses only dried materials, the sand may be dry also.

Miniatures may be made the same way, and are pretty for a breakfast tray, a small bedside table, or for a May gift. Use a metal jar top, or waxed container top, or a pretty little cup and saucer for the container. A bit of florist clay will hold dried materials in place, and moist sand or Oasis will hold those that need moisture.

Insect Cage

The easiest and quickest way to observe an insect closely is to pop it into a cage and keep it there just long enough to get a really good look at it. The easiest way to make a quickie cage is to take a bit of screening about six by twelve inches in size, roll it into a cylinder, and fit it snugly into a jar lid for a base. Sew or tape the edges of the cylinder, add another jar lid for the top—and there you are! Observe your insect visitors—then release them.

Bird, Tree or Flower Inventory

It is interesting to keep a record of all the birds seen at the feeding station, or on walks; or to list the wildflowers found, or the trees that have been identified. A very good and impressive way to do this is also very simple. Just hang an old, white windowshade on a door or wall. Then, with a heavy pen or magic marker, record each object as it is identified. Keep separate records, or divide the windowshade into sections, label each, and keep several inventories at once.

Bird Caller

The *easiest* way to call birds is merely to kiss the back of your hand with a loud, squeaky, long kiss! It must sound a bit like a young bird in trouble—or else the birds are curious to see what made that queer sound.

A very effective caller can be made, however, and carried in the pocket. Its use will help to lure the birds closer to you, so that you can get a better view of them.

Find a piece of hardwood about two inches long and an inch in diameter. A bit of an old hammer handle, other tool handle, or broomstick will do.

Get a screweye large enough to be turned easily with the fingers. Drill a hole in one end of the wood, making it a bit *smaller* than the thread of the screweye. Turn the screweye into the hole, then remove it. Sprinkle a bit of resin into the hole. Then try turning the screweye back and forth in the hole. It will make a penetrating, squeaky sound, and will lure the birds a bit nearer to see what makes it.

Don't expect the birds to flock to you when you use this birdcaller. Keep very still and quiet. Wait a bit between squeaks, and watch carefully. It is very likely you will see the movement of birds in the trees as they try to identify the sound.

Spiderweb Print

When made with care, and properly mounted, this print will be so interesting that you will want to frame it.

First find a suitable web. Look for it among bushes or weeds in the morning when the dew is on it. It will show up better then, and you can get a clearer view of the lovely pattern it makes. Note the web itself. Its lines that go round and round are slightly sticky, to help hold any insect that gets into the web. Notice the "guy lines" that hold the web in place. They are not sticky, and the spider uses them for runways when it goes to capture the insect in the web.

Later, when the web has dried out, go back to make the print. Chase the spider away from it, being very careful not to touch the web. Have someone hold a big shield of newspapers behind the web. Then, very carefully, spray it on both sides, but lightly, with white enamel (or other color if you prefer. White just looks more natural). Use great care, and don't work too close to the net. You don't want the net to sag with the weight of the paint.

When the net is completely sprayed, put a piece of black construction paper behind the web. Very carefully, bring it into contact with the web so that the web will stick to the paper. Then cut those guy lines that anchor the net to the bushes or weeds. Now you have your web safely on paper. Let it dry thoroughly—then look at it and marvel at one of nature's masterpieces.

Mushroom Print

Find and bring back, very carefully, a full-grown mushroom. Cut off the stem. Place the mushroom cap, gills down, on a piece of paper. Cover it with a glass or bowl so that it won't get moved, or jarred, or windblown. In the morning, lift off the covering very carefully, and remove the mushroom, also with great care. And then you will see the mushroom print. The lines of the gill will show up as clear places, and the mushroom spores will be in a lovely, rayed pattern.

Some mushrooms have black spores. Others have spores of various colors—white, yellow, pink, brown, rust. Select the color of paper that will contrast best with the color of the spores of the mushroom you use—if you can tell. You may have to experiment with a few. Black paper will show up white spores the best, and white paper will contrast best with black spores.

To make the print more permanent, if you wish to, put a very thin coating of glue mixed with water over the paper before putting the mushroom on it. Or spray the paper with a light plastic paint. Then use broken matchsticks to hold the mushroom very slightly off the paper, so the mushroom won't stick to the paper, cover it with bowl or glass, and proceed as above. The shadow of the matchsticks may show on the print, but it will still be lovely.

PART IV

Crafts From
Nature's Pantry Shelf

Something To Look For

Nature is as near at hand as the pantry shelf, the vegetable bin, the kitchen table! Many of nature's greatest gifts are the things we take for granted—the fruits that we eat with relish, the vegetables that we serve cooked or raw, the spices and herbs that make our meals taste better. Many come from far away—but they are as close to us as the nearest supermarket or grocery store. In fact, the supermarket and grocery store can be a real nature center for adults and children. Look for the many fruits. Learn to identify them all by name. Notice their shapes, the texture of their skins, their smells. Some, like oranges and lemons, have a textured surface. Some, like plums, grapes and apples, have smooth skins. Some, like some varieties of pears, have warty skins. Others, like bananas, have skins like soft leather. And some, like pineapples, have a patterned, rough skin like an alligator.

Look for the different kinds of *melons*. Notice the differences in size, the shades of coloring, the delicate lacework on the skins. Find out the names of the different varieties, and call them by name.

The experience of watching a garden grow and ripen, then the picking of the produce, is the very best way to get to know how vegetables grow and what they are like as they grow. If a vegetable garden is not possible, then the grocery store, the vegetable stand and the supermarket will provide excellent ways to get acquainted with nature's pantry shelf.

Study the long bins of the fruits and vegetables. After buying the family supply, provide extra experiences of touching, smelling, tasting, helping to prepare, and helping to cook the food.

Look for the spice shelves and learn the names that sound romantic and strange—oregano, nutmeg, mace, cloves, saffron, paprika, cinnamon, allspice, curry, pepper.

Among the spices may be the *herbs*, some native, some from far away. The *mints* will be there. Such a big family! In it are marjoram, savory, thyme, rosemary, spearmint, pennyroyal and sage. They'll all taste different, and they all add flavor to our vegetables, meats, salads and desserts.

All of these spices and herbs came from *plants*. Look to see what part of the plant was used—the seeds, bark, flowers, roots, or leaves. Sometimes the spice or herb will be all ground up, but often its original form will also be on the shelf. Look for it. Look for the big, wooden-like nutmegs, the large, flat bayleaves, cinnamon bark, whole peppercorns, whole coffee beans.

Look for ways to explain how plants grow—the sprouting potato, the carrot tops, the sprouting onion, the strange-looking pineapple with its stiff top. Cut some of these open, and look for the pretty seed arrangements. Cut a thin slice of potato crosswise. Hold it up to the light and see the pretty star inside.

Look for strange and amusing shapes in fruits and vegetables. Encourage the child to use his imagination and his sense of humor by turning some of these into animal shapes or funny figures. Kitchen chores can be turned into play by such projects—and the results can always be eaten!

Look for ways to make food and food products interesting. Visit a potato farm, or a truck garden. Look at a field of cabbages—such a pretty sight. Visit a cannery. Go to a botanical garden and see how some of the tropical plants grow—what a pineapple plant looks like, how the bunch of bananas seems to grow upside down, what a coffee flower looks like before the berry forms.

Look at the *colors* in the familiar fruits and vegetables. Look for designs. Encourage the child to become aware of the beauty of these familiar things, and to enjoy their looks as well as their smell and taste.

Look for labels that tell where the vegetable or fruit came from—potatoes from Maine, Idaho, Long Island; apples from Oregon, Washington, New York; okra from Louisiana; melons from Georgia; oranges from Florida, Texas, California. A meal can be a real travel adventure.

76

Something To Talk About

The FOOD we eat.
Which are *roots?*

Beets	Carrots	Radishes
Turnips	Parsnips	Salsify

Which are *stems?*

Rhubarb	Leeks
Celery	Asparagus

Which are *leaves?*

Spinach	Lettuce	Parsley
Endive	Cabbage	Kale
Watercress	Swiss Chard	

Which are really the *buds* of plants?

Cauliflower	Broccoli	Brussels Sprouts

What vegetables we eat are really *fruits* of a plant?

Stringbeans	Peas	Pumpkin
Eggplant	Rice	Peppers
Lima beans	Okra	Corn
Squash	Tomatoes	Cucumber

What *sap* do we eat?

Maple sugar	Sugar cane	Beet sugar

What *seeds* do we drink?

Coffee	Cocoa

What *leaf* do we drink?

Tea

What Foods Taste Like

Taste them and see. Talk about words for taste:

peppery	bitter	nutty	bland
sweet	spicy	sour	starchy

Suppose someone had never seen or tasted such vegetables as:

Cabbage	Cauliflower	Beets	Carrots
Tomatoes	Celery	Onions	Asparagus

What words would you use to describe how they look and taste?

77

Where Foods Come From

Talk about the origins of foods.

Asparagus has been eaten as food in Europe for two thousand years. Its name means "to swell, or be ripe"—just what those fat stems do.

Beans are fairly new, compared to many plants. They were first cultivated in North and South America only three or four hundred years ago. *Stringbeans* are the oldest. They were introduced into Europe by the Spanish explorers back in the last part of the 15th century, *Lima beans* soon after. Beans are of two types—those that we eat for the pods, such as stringbeans, and those we eat for the bean, such as kidney beans and lima beans.

Beets originated in the Canary Islands and around the Mediterranean. They have been known for around two thousand years. Their name comes from the Greek "Beta", the second letter of the Greek alphabet, because the Greeks thought the seeds resembled the shape of that letter. Look at a beet seed and see if it does.

Broccoli comes from western Asia and has been known for over two thousand years. Its popularity, though, is fairly recent.

Cabbage has been eaten as a food for over four thousand years. It first came from western Asia.

Carrots, originally from the temperate parts of Asia, have been known for two thousand years.

Cauliflower, from western Asia, has been known for two thousand years.

Celery grew wild in Europe. It was cultivated around the 17th century.

Sweet Corn was cultivated by the American Indians in both North and South America long before the early colonists came, or America was discovered. The Indians showed the colonists how to cultivate and cook it, and it helped to keep them from starving during their first years.

Watercress has been known for centuries. It probably first originated in Persia.

Cucumbers are native to southern Asia. They have been cultivated for some four thousand years.

Eggplants have been eaten as food in India for several thousand years.

Endive originated in Egypt in very early times.

Kale was first known in Europe, several thousand years ago.

Leeks come from the Mediterranean area. They have been used for food since pre-historic times.

Muskmelons originated in either Africa or Asia. They were not cultivated, however, until the Christian era.

Okra, whose pods look like small green bananas, was brought to the United States from Africa by the slave trade in the 18th century. It now grows in the southern states where it is used to thicken soups and gumbos.

Onions, along with *turnips* and *radishes,* are the oldest vegetables known. The onion probably originated in Asia. It was grown by the ancient Egyptians. Legend says that the slaves building the Great Pyramid once went on strike because onions had been left out of their food. Shallots, chives and garlic are close relatives to the onion.

Parsley grew wild in southern Europe. It is so old and so well-known that it was mentioned as a vegetable in Charlemagne's garden.

Peas, native of Europe, have been grown since early times.

Peppers are native to South America, and have been cultivated for centuries.

Potatoes are also natives of South America, and were found there by the Spanish explorers in the latter part of the 16th century. North American Indians also grew them. Sir Walter Raleigh learned how to use them from the Indians, and sent them to England. The potato in those days was a small, nubbly thing. Its present form is due to improved techniques of cultivation.

Pumpkins are so old that their rinds have been found on the sites of the ancient Swiss Lake Dwellers.

Radish, which means "root", is a native of western Asia, but has spread so widely that its exact origin is unknown. With the onion and the turnip, it is the oldest known vegetable.

Rhubarb was discovered in southern Siberia in Christian times.

Spinach probably first grew in Persia. It was introduced into Europe in the 15th century.

Squash is a native of tropical America. It was first discovered in 1490.

Tomatoes were first eaten as food in Peru. In Colonial America, tomatoes were thought to be poisonous, and they were raised only for their green foliage and red fruits. They were called "love apples" in those days.

Turnips, with onions and radishes, share the honor of being the world's oldest vegetables. It has been in cultivation more than four thousand years.

What Our Drinks Are Made Of

Chocolate or Cocoa comes from the ground-up, roasted cacao bean. Cacao trees are native to South America, and the South American Indians have made chocolate drinks for centuries. The trees are now grown in Mexico, the West Indies, etc. The seeds are in a big pod. They are dried and partly fermented before use.

Tea is made from the leaves, leaf buds and internodes of a shrub that is grown in India, China and Japan. Look at the label to see what kind of tea it is:

> *Green tea*—the leaves are picked, rolled and dried at once.
>
> *Black tea*—the leaves are fermented and oxidized before drying.
>
> *Oolong tea*—the leaves are partly fermented and oxidized before drying.

Coffee comes from the seeds of a berry-like fruit of a small tree or shrub. The seeds are red. The dark brown color of the coffee bean occurs because the seeds are roasted. The flowers of the coffee tree are small, white, and fragrant. Look for coffee beans in the supermarket, before they are ground. Nibble one.

Spices and Herbs

Food would be very flat and uninteresting if we had no seasonings to give it flavor. In olden days, spices and herbs were even more important. With no refrigeration, food spoiled quickly. Spices and herbs helped to preserve the food, and to hide the spoiled taste. With no modern plumbing, and without the same standards of sanitation and cleanliness, homes and people were very likely to smell disagreeably. Here again spices and herbs played a part in hiding the bad smells.

Most big estates and monasteries had their own extensive herb gardens. Herbs were used not only for cooking and flavoring, but as medicines and cosmetics as well.

Spices were the main reasons for many of the early explorations. The big sailing ships hoped to get to the Spice Islands to bring back cargoes of spice, to be sold for large profits. The spice trade was behind much of the early European colonization in the Pacific, and the Far East.

The canned or bottled herbs and spices found on the shelves of grocery stores and supermarkets may include mostly the pulverized kinds, but look for some of the original forms. Cinnamon, for example, is a *bark*. Buy a bit at a drugstore, and chew it!

Allspice is a berry of a tree that belongs to the myrtle family.

Aniseed is the seed of the anise flower. It belongs to the carrot family. It is the flavor for licorice.

Basil is the dried leaves of the basil plant. It originated in western Europe. It is popular for salads and for tomato dishes.

Bay Leaves are from a wild shrub of the eastern Mediterranean area. A relative of it grows on the west coast.

Cinnamon is the bark of a tree that belongs to the laurel family, growing in the Orient.

Cloves are dried flower buds of a tropical tree, also of the myrtle family.

Dill also is the seed of a plant that belongs to the carrot family. It gives a special flavor to pickles. It is European.

Carraway Seed is also a member of the carrot family. It is imported from Holland.

Curry is a blend of many spices. It has been used for centuries in India and other Eastern countries. It gives food such a hot flavor that the people eating it don't notice the hot climate!

Ginger comes from the ground-up root of a plant that grows in Asia and Polynesia.

Mace is the dried pulp around the nutmeg kernel. It has a nutmeg smell and taste.

Mints, like the members of the carrot family, come in many flavors. The mint plants all have distinctive, four-sided stems and two-lipped flowers, and they are all very aromatic. *Savory* from France and Spain, *rosemary* from southern Europe and Asia Minor, *marjoram* from France and Chile, are all members of the mint family. So are *thyme* and *sage. Pennyroyal,* a mint, can be rubbed on the body to ward off mosquitoes. *Spearmint* is used to flavor candy and chewing gum, among other things.

Oregano is made from the dried leaves of a plant native to Italy and Mexico.

Pepper is the most widely used of all the spices. It comes from the berry, called peppercorn, that grows on a vine. This vine climbs about twenty feet high. Each vine can produce about five pounds of pepper a year.

The berries for *black pepper* are picked before they are ripe, while they are still a yellowish-green. They are dried until the outside skin shrivels, hardens and turns black. Berries of *white pepper* are picked when fully ripe and red. They are soaked to loosen the outer skins, then sun-dried.

Pepper comes from India, Indonesia and Malaysia. It is best when it is ground fresh when used. Many people keep pepper grinders on the dining table.

Saffron is the most expensive of all the spices. It comes from a form of crocus with a purple flower. It is the dried stigma of that flower—and it takes many of them to make even a small amount of saffron. Saffron is used to flavor food, and to give it a yellow color.

Something To Make

Hands can be busy while adult and child share information about the surprising things that come from nature's pantry shelf, from both home and supermarket. Many projects can be made just for fun. Others can be made for surprises, for birthdays, for holidays. They provide good ways to say "I love you".

As with other nature crafts, the emphasis should be put on *nature* rather than on any finished product. Make adventures out of finding, collecting, identifying and using. What is finally produced as a result will be far more rewarding and worthwhile.

Jack-O-Lanterns

These are child-sized, and little Scottish and Irish boys and girls have made them for centuries.

No big pumpkins! These are made of apples and turnips. Hollow out the apple or turnip. Use nuts or bits of wood or cloves for teeth and eyes. Insert a small carrot or pickle for a nose. Make Jack into

APPLE   TURNIP

Jack-o-lanterns

a human head, or an animal head. Let each child make his own small jack-o-lantern. A small candle or flashlight will make it even more eerie as a table decoration.

To display one or more of these jacks, make a small base of wood and fasten dowel sticks several inches along its length. Push the sticks, sharpened if necessary, up into the apples or turnips. An even easier way is to hammer some nails in the board, then impale the apples or turnips on them, to hold them neatly in a row.

Kitchen Kreatures

These are the quickies, the fun things to make while Mother is preparing a meal. They make for good child-talk, for getting the "feel" of fruits, vegetables, nuts and other foods. The projects here are all simple, and can be varied to suit the child's own imagination.

Peanut Pete. His hat is the cap from a tube of toothpaste, glued on. His hands and feet are pipecleaners, pushed through holes that have been punched carefully, so as not to split the peanut. Paint eyes, nose and mouth. Make one for every member of the family.

Peanut Puppets. Cut peanut shells in half, removing the peanuts (and eating them!). Paint or draw a funny face on each half-shell. Add a paper hat on some of them, glueing it to the shell. Then put a peanut puppet on each finger of the hand, and put on a puppet act.

82

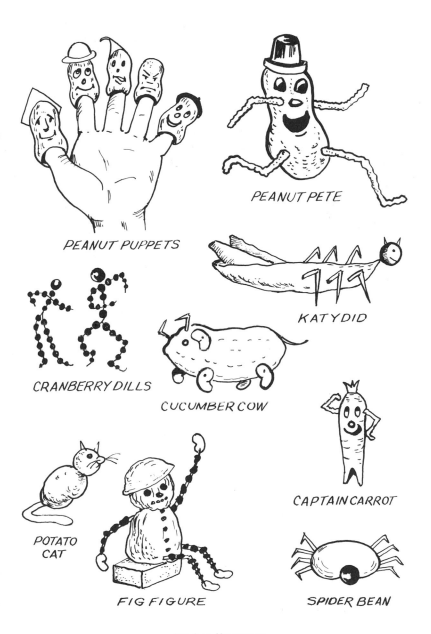

PEANUT PUPPETS

PEANUT PETE

KATYDID

CRANBERRY DILLS

CUCUMBER COW

CAPTAIN CARROT

POTATO CAT

FIG FIGURE

SPIDER BEAN

Kitchen Kreatures

Peanut Animals. Some unshelled peanuts already look a bit like camels, or buffaloes, or other animals. Add toothpicks or matchsticks for legs, a straw or bit of pipecleaner for a tail. Paint or decorate as desired.

Carrot Puppet. Somewhat similar to Peanut Puppets, but much larger. Cut off the base of a large carrot, then scrape out a hole up into the carrot big enough to fit the index finger. Draw or scrape features on the top end of the carrot for the face. Cut the carrot-top leaves into a crew cut, or spread them downward for long hair. Drape a big handkerchief or paper towel over the index finger, and insert the finger into the hole. The handkerchief will form the puppet's dress. Then—put on a Carrot Show.

Cranberry Dancing Dolls. String cranberries on fine wires that can be bent into figure shapes. Bend the wire at the ends, so the berries won't fall off. Then bend the wire into figures in various poses. These make pretty decorations for a Christmas tree, too.

Cucumber Cow. Pick out a shortish, plump cucumber for the body. Fasten on lima bean ears, and toothpick legs. Use bits of bent toothpicks for horns.

Captain Carrot. Select a tall, straight, sturdy carrot. Cut a wedge out of the bottom of the carrot to indicate legs. If the Captain won't stand on these legs, brace it with toothpicks. Insert pipecleaners for arms. Paint on the facial features and the uniform, or use strips of green pepper to indicate the tunic, and cloves for buttons.

Porcupine Turnip. Select a nice, round turnip for the body. Stick lots of toothpicks in the body to make Porky's quills. Add a matchstick for the tail and burnt matches for legs and eyes.

Apple Funny Face. Select a big, firm apple. Use a marshmallow for a cap, a gumdrop for a nose, and a long strip of gumdrop for the mouth. Fasten these on with toothpicks or wire hairpins.

Katydid. Select a long, full peapod for the body. Split another pea and remove the seeds. Use one of the peas for a head. The two halves of the pod form the wings. Then split a short, wide pod in half. Fasten half of it across the back of the katydid with six bent toothpicks for legs. Use short bits of a toothpick for the feelers.

Potato Cat. Find a small potato with a little nubbin on one end, or use a large and a small potato, pinned together with a toothpick. These form the body and head of the cat. Cut two small ears and a long tail out of cardboard. Make slits in the potatoes and insert the ears and tail. Whiskers can be cut from a broom. Cloves make good eyes.

Spider Bean. Use a fat, round lima bean for the body. Bend eight toothpicks and insert them for legs. Fasten on a small pea for a head.

Prune Boy. His head is an English walnut, or a prune, or a fig.

His body is made of two prunes. Two more prunes, rolled into a longer shape, make his arms. Fasten them on with toothpicks or matchsticks. Add bits of gumdrops, or bits of other fruits or vegetables to make his facial features. Brace Prune Boy with toothpicks so that he will sit in position.

Fig Figure. His body is a fig pulled into shape. His head is two dried prunes pressed together to form a ball. Arms and legs are raisins strung on four toothpicks. His hands and feet are shelled almonds or lima beans. Eyes, nose, mouth and coat buttons are cloves. His hat is half a walnut shell. Sit Fig Boy on a lump of sugar and use for a place favor.

Grapefruit and Orange Rind

These rinds make nice little bowls, dishes, baskets and candleholders. Peel the meat from the fruit (and eat it!). Then decide upon the shape you want. For one shape, scrape off the pulp, put a water goblet inside the rind, and press the peel up around it, being careful not to split or break the rind. Leave it that way to dry out thoroughly. Then—a pretty little hard bowl for paperclips or matches.

Or flatten the peel around a small bowl, so that the rind will dry in a low, flattish shape. Then use as a little candleholder.

Apple-head Dolls

This is a project that can be just for fun, or, when done with great care, can produce some remarkable effects.

Peel an apple, scoop out bits of one side to barely suggest features—hollows for eyes, along the nose, etc. Nature will do most of the rest. Place the apple head on wax paper in a cool, dry place so that it will dry out and not rot. The head will shrivel and take on quite life-like features. You can add to the effect by slightly pinching up the nose, and slightly modeling the features with your fingers as the apple dries.

Attach the head to a plastic bottle. The ones that look body-shaped are the best. For an Indian doll, give the face a bit of war paint and add some scrap of cloth for an Indian blanket. Add yarn hair, braiding it and pinning the braid on with a straight pin. Use cloves for eyes.

For a *Granny Doll* prepare the apple as above. When it has dried, slightly color the lips, eyebrows and cheeks. Add blue-headed pins for eyes, or use cloves.

Give Granny a body made out of part of a nylon stocking stuffed with cotton or other old stockings, or foam rubber. Dress her in black or lavender, and give her a little ruffle of lace at her throat. Add a bit of lace for a cap, if you like. Granny's hair is yarn in smooth strands, wound into a coil and pulled away from her face.

Embroidery floss can also be used for hair. Add rice for teeth, if you like.

As the apples for these dolls dry, they become withered and wrinkled, making very, very interesting, old-aged faces.

Other types of bodies can be devised. A wire coathanger, for example, can be straightened out, then bent in the middle. The bent end can be stuck up into the apple head, leaving the two ends to form the body and legs of the doll. Another wire can be bent around the coathanger wire, up under the apple, to make the arms. Then the doll can be padded and dressed.

These apple dolls were made for little girls by the early colonists when toys were scarce and parents had to make them for the children, using whatever was at hand.

Easter Eggs

All children love to make colored Easter eggs, and are familiar with the usual dyes and decals available from a store. Try a few *nature* ways.

Collect a handful of ferns, fold them around the eggs tightly, and tie them with a piece of cheesecloth drawn tight and tied around the eggs. Boil the eggs until hardboiled, then let them sit in the hot water about ten minutes. When unwrapped, the eggs will have a pretty, pale, fern design.

Use the same method with red onionskins to get a pretty red egg; with yellow onionskins for yellow eggs.

Egg Scenes are pleasant variations. With a sharp-pointed nail scissor, bore and chip out carefully a small hole in the broad side of the egg, making it about an inch or so in diameter, so that it forms a small window. Carefully empty out the egg contents, and rinse the shell out carefully. Find a pretty little Easter scene of flowers, bunnies, chicks, or use tiny miniature figures, such as small, fluffy baby chicks made of cotton. When the shell is thoroughly dry, glue the little scene or figures inside. They will be pretty on an Easter Egg Tree.

Easter Egg Trees are an old Polish tradition worth keeping alive. To decorate a tree, the eggs must be light in weight, and so must be blown out. To blow out an egg, carefully chip out a hole in the egg at both ends. Poke in a long pin or needle to break the egg yolk, then blow at one end, holding the other end over a dish to catch the contents of the egg. The two holes need not be tiny. They can be about a quarter of an inch in diameter, because they can be covered with masking tape. When the eggs have been blown out and rinsed, decorate them with scraps of felt, or paper glued on in pretty designs, or with fancy tape or stick-ons, or with paint. Cover one of the holes with a bit of masking tape. Do the same with the other hole, but first put a knotted length of string through the tape so the egg can be tied to the tree.

The Easter Egg Tree is any well-shaped branch, bare of leaves, set in a flowerpot or vase so that it will stand securely. Hang the eggs to the various twigs of the tree, and use the Easter Egg Tree as a decoration throughout the Easter season, or for the Easter Day family dinner.

The "tree" may be sprayed white or any pastel color before decorating, if you like. Very gay and pretty.

Nature Dyes

Try dyeing eggs, cotton cloth, yarn, linen mats, scarves or other articles, using natural dye materials. Here are a few colors that are possible. Experiment with others.

Tea gives a lovely, pale ecru to a dark, reddish brown, depending upon the strength of the tea.

Coffee yields shades of brown, depending upon the strength of the coffee.

Onionskins give you two choices—red onionskins for a red color, yellow onionskins for a yellow color.

Beets make a pretty reddish-purple.

Blackberries make a blue dye. Remove the seeds.

Raspberries make a dark red color.

Strawberries make a lighter, pinkish red.

Spinach makes a yellow-green.

In Colonial days, and in Civil War days, women used all sorts of natural materials for dyeing the family clothing and household goods:

Sumac berries for a dark, good, brownish-red
Walnut hulls for a dark, deep brown
Dandelion roots for a bright, light purple
Sassafras roots for a pretty pink
Butternut bark for a good brown
Pokeweed berries for a strong purple
Goldenrod flowers for a dull yellow

Watch Things Grow

One of the easiest ways to watch a *seed sprout* is to use a clear glass. Soak several dried lima beans in water overnight. Then fill a water glass with soil and plant the beans up against the sides of the glass, so that they are visible from the outside. Keep the soil moist, and cover the glass with a paper towel for several days. Then look at it. The little root can be seen, pushing down into the soil, and before long, up will climb the first leaves!

Try this method with grapefruit or orange seeds, too, but be sure that the seeds are from a fully developed, ripe fruit, otherwise they won't grow.

Carrot Tops are fun to grow. Cut the head off the carrot, leaving about an inch at the top. Put it in a bowl or dish of sand, vermiculite or other rooting material, leaving the carrot top exposed but partly buried. Keep the rooting mixture moist and in a shady place. In about a week, up will come some leaves, green and fresh.

Try this same method with a beet.

Another method to use with a carrot is to cut off the bottom of a long carrot about a third of the way up. Scoop out a good part of the bottom of the carrot. Punch holes on either side of the scooped out part, run a cord through them, and hang the carrot up. It will be upside down. Fill the scooped area with water, and keep it filled. Pretty green leaves will start growing out at the bottom, and will curve upward.

Green Potato Pigs are fun to watch. Scoop out part of a large potato. Add matchstick legs and a tail, thumbtacked on. Fill the hole in the potato with an inch or so of garden soil, moisten, and seed with grass seed. Very soon the potato pig will have a green back. Keep the grass cut with scissors.

Gourds

Gourds are fascinating. They come in all sizes, shapes and colors. In the fall, stop at a roadside stand, and let the child explore the gourds on display. Buy a dozen or so, and plan to make a *Fiesta Charm String* for the patio, front door, fireplace or playroom.

The best gourds for this purpose are the ones with necks. Pick out different sizes, shapes and colors. Take them home, and wash them in warm, soapy water to remove all soil. Then rinse them well in water to which a few drops of household disinfectant have been added. Dry them well with a soft cloth, being very careful not to bruise or nick them.

Then set them on newspapers, not touching each other, in a dry, airy place. Turn them over once in a while, and change any moist paper. If a gourd shows signs of decay, develops any mold or soft spots, discard it at once. Let the others dry out thoroughly for three or four weeks.

With an auger or drill, drill holes across the necks, so that the gourds can be wired or tied into the Charm String. Add other natural materials, such as dried red peppers, bittersweet, locust pods, etc., blending them for shape and color. Tie all of these materials into the strands of a rope, using wire or heavy cord to hold them in place. Leave a loop of the rope for hanging the string where you want it. These are very decorative, and can add a spot of autumn color to wherever they are placed.

88

Gourd Birds are fun to make if you live in a warm section of the country where you can get the large, hard, thin-shelled gourds.

Find a gourd with a long, curved neck, looking like the neck of a big bird. Dry it out as above. Then drill two holes for legs and a hole for the beak. Insert two sticks or dowels whittled to fit the leg holes. Insert a sharp-pointed stick for a beak. Then paint the bird in wild, gay, Mexican colors.

These big, hard-shelled gourds can be sawed into various shapes for use as cups, bowls, and dippers. They have been used for such purposes by people of the tropics for hundreds of years.

Potato Prints

Cut a good-sized potato in half, and put the cut sides down on a piece of paper toweling so that their moisture can be absorbed, keeping them there for several hours before using. This will make the potato much more solid and will give you better prints.

Then trace a design—a little flower, a leaf, a bird, or an abstract design onto the cut surface of the potato. With a pocket knife or sharp paring knife, cut away the potato from around the design, leaving the design standing up. Don't undercut any of the lines.

Press the design onto an inkpad or plastic sponge holding poster paint. Don't push it in too deep. You want just the design to be in the paint. Then press the paint side firmly against the article to be painted—notepaper, table mat, book cover, apron, or such. When printing fabrics, special fabric dye should be used so the article can be washed without fading.

Do the entire potato print job at one time. The potato won't last. It will turn black and soft if kept too long.

Open Fruit Basket

A handsome decoration for table or mantel. Makes a good holiday decoration.

Buy a fifteen-inch square of hardware cloth (heavy screening) from the hardware store. It is very inexpensive. Bind all four sides with two- and a half-inch floral ribbon. Buy the ribbon in a florist shop. The velour type is the prettiest. Any good glue, such as Elmer's, Sobo, Nuglu, etc., will hold the ribbon binding into place.

When the ribbon binding is in place and dry, hold the wire by diagonal corners, and bring them up until the tips overlap just a bit. Fasten them together with a brass brad. It will go easily through the ribbon and the wire. Tie a big bow over the brad, at the top of the basket. It will take a yard of ribbon.

Fill the basket with fruit, cones, pine branches, or other holiday materials—perhaps gourds and bittersweet for Thanksgiving. It will look somewhat like a big cornucopia, open at both ends, and spilling out beauty.

Fruit or Flower Tier

A fruit or flower bowl on three levels makes a very striking decoration. This one is inexpensive to make, and looks very unique.

All it takes is two small, three-inch flowerpots to provide the height, and three flowerpot saucers in graduated sizes, eleven inch, seven and a half inches, and four inches in diameter.

Paint the pots and saucers a flat black. Then give them a coat of emerald mist green, but wipe off the green while it is still wet, so that the post and saucers get an antique iron shade.

Glue the first pot upside down in the center of the largest saucer. Then glue the next largest saucer to the bottom of that pot. Finally, glue the rim of the second pot to the center of that saucer, and glue the smallest saucer on top of it. You now have a three-tiered bowl. Next comes the decorating of it.

Fill the saucers with dabs of glued, dry styrofoam. Then glue pieces of artificial fruits and leaves into the saucers. Floral adhesive will work, but it sets very fast. Small bunches of grapes, plums, cherries, limes and other fairly small fruits look the best. Let some of them hang over the edges in some places.

Of course *real* fruit will look even prettier, but it will have to be replaced as it is eaten or grows old. In using real fruit, omit the styrofoam.

Flowers, nuts, vines, and other natural materials can be used and will look lovely. Artificial flowers can be used if styrofoam is glued into the saucers.

A small figurine of some sort, perhaps a bird, antiqued to match the bowl and glued on the top, can be added and will look very decorative.

PART V

Crafts From Nature's Flowerbeds

Something To Look For

Flowers

The big, beautiful flowers in gardens. The less familiar flowers in the florist shop and in the botanical garden. Flowers that bloom in the spring. Indoor flowers. Flowers that bloom along the railroad tracks and the city dump. Flowers of the woods and those of the sunny fields. Hard-to-see flowers of the trees in the spring. Tiny flowers on the grasses.

Look for the stamens and pistils in flowers. The stamens carry the pollen and are the male part that fertilizes the pistils, or the female part of the flower that holds the ovary. Flowers often depend upon bees, butterflies and other insects to scatter the pollen so that the ovary is fertilized, and can make seeds to produce new plants.

Look for colors in flowers. How many reds can be seen? Yellows? Blues? Pinks? Whites? Some flower books are arranged by color to help in quick identification.

Smell flowers. Which ones are fragrant? Some will smell spicy, like the pinks and carnations and stock. Some will smell sweet, like roses and clover. Some will be very aromatic, like all of the mints. Some will be very strongly sweet, like the gardenia, and jasmine, and the linden tree blossoms that can be smelled blocks away.

Touch flowers. Sometimes the petals will feel velvety, like those of the rose. Sometimes they feel like thin silk, like the poppy's petals. Sometimes there will be prickles nearby, as with the thistle.

Look for look-alikes. Flowers, like people, have families. A lovely garden flower may have a relative that grows wild in the fields. One member of the family may be cherished; a relative may be a weed.

These will have a family resemblance. For example, all the members of the big mint family have square stems and a strong, aromatic smell.

The lovely lilies all have six petal-like parts, and the leaves grow up the stem. That stately calla lily that you see at Easter can't be a lily. It lacks those six petal-like parts and its leaves are all at the bottom. It belongs to the Arum family, and is first cousin to the jack-in-the-pulpit. Note the lance-shaped leaves growing from the base, very different from the real lily's foliage. The flower of the calla lily really isn't a flower at all. It is very special *leaf*. The real flowers are inside, and are very tiny.

Notice the *shapes* of flowers. Some are many-petaled, like the daisies. Look carefully and find two kinds of flowers in a daisy. Those outside petals are called "rays". Inside, look for the tiny "disk" flowers. Such flowers as the daisy are called composite.

Some flowers have umbrella-shaped heads, called "umbrels," made up of hundreds of tiny flowers. Queen Anne's lace is one of them.

Some have trumpet-shaped flowers, sometimes like tubes, sometimes more bell-shaped. Some have three flower parts, or multiples of three. These shapes help us to find out what big family the flower belongs to.

The great rose family has flowers with five petals, and stamens in a circle around a cup-shaped part. The many-petaled roses of our gardens have been grown on rootstocks of the real rose, and have been hybridized so that the circle of stamens has become extra petals. The common little wild cinquefoil is a relative. Look at its five petals in a little cap.

The big mustard family has flowers with four petals. Its botanical name means "cross-bearers," because those petals look like a little cross. Our hot vegetables, such as watercress, mustard and radishes all belong to this family. So does stock, that is so spicily fragrant, and the sweet-smelling candytuft and sweet alyssum. Look at the tiny flowers, and see if you can recognize the family likeness.

The botanical name of the widespread buttercup family means "little frog", because all the members of that family like to have their feet wet. They all carry a cluster of seedpods or a ball of seeds, but in size, color and shape the members can look very different. Marsh-marigolds belong to this family. So do pasque flowers, anemones, larkspur, peony, clematis and many others.

The iris family has a name that means "like a horseback rider" because of the way the leaves grow, one on top of another. The word "iris" means "rainbow", and it is easy to guess why when you look at the many colors. Gladiolas belong to this family. So do freesias and the crocus.

The pea family is one of the largest of them all. Its botanical name means "pod". We eat many of the pea family, either for the pods or for the peas inside. Most of this family have flowers with very similar forms. Look at the flower of a sweet pea, or the blossom of a stringbean. The lupines belong to this family. So do the blue bonnets of Texas, the peanut, the clovers and wisteria. Big or tiny, their flowers are all shaped alike. The pea family produces nodules on its roots, and these enrich the soil they grow on.

The *Flower Family Album* and *Recognizing Flowering Wild Plants* (see RESOURCES) are excellent guides to flower families.

Something To Talk About

What ARE Flowers?

Not every plant has flowers, in fact, two-thirds of the plants of the world are non-flowering. How dreary the world would be, however, if there were no flowers.

Flowering plants are those that over the centuries have learned how to reproduce themselves by *seeds*. Their whole system works for that purpose. Their colors, their smells, and their shapes are developed to attract bees, butterflies and other insects so that the plants may be pollinated and so be able to form seeds that will grow into new plants.

The seeds are meant to be distributed. Some, like those of the jewelweed or touch-me-not, pop out quite a distance when they are ripe. Some, like those of the dandelion, have parachutes to take them great distances in the wind. Poppies have seeds in a seedpod that is like a salt shaker. The tiny seeds are shaken out when the wind blows the pod, or when it breaks.

Some seeds grow in pods, some in capsules. Some are very smooth; others are so barbed that they can hook onto anything that gets near, such as the fur of an animal or the trousers of a man.

Some are so tiny that they have to be mixed with sand when sown, like the petunia seeds. Some are very flat and thin, like zinnia seeds. Take a good look at various kinds of seeds and note how functional as well as beautiful they are.

Where Do Flowers COME From?

A flower may not move from its place in the garden or field, but its family very probably were great travelers in the past—and are still traveling. Every early colonist or settler took along some packets of seeds when he and his family moved—seeds for crops, and seeds for flowers.

Wars help to distribute plants and flowers. Every soldier remembers his home and his garden, and often brings back samples or seeds of interesting plants he has seen on his trip. The men in the early Crusades brought back or sent back to England and to Europe many flowers and plants they found in the Mediterranean and Levant areas.

Explorers also were a big help in distributing plants. Cortez and his troops discovered and took away many plants and seeds from Mexico. The flower, Clarkia, is named after William Clark, of the Lewis and Clark Expedition.

How Do Flowers Get Their Names?

Flowers get their names all sorts of ways! Sometimes they are named for a *place,* like Pride of London, a name given to Bouncing Bet. Sometimes they are named for the person who first cultivated them. Forsythia, for example, was named for William Forsyth, gardener to King George III. Bougainvillea was named for Louis de Bougainville, the first Frenchman to cross the Pacific, and the man who found the beautiful vine growing in Rio de Janeiro. Dahlias were named for the Swedish botanist, Andreas Dahl.

The same flowers are often called by all sorts of local names in other parts of the world. This made identification very difficult until the great Carolus Linnaeus, a Swedish naturalist, brought order in 1735 by setting up a world-accepted system by which each plant got *two* names, a big, family name, and its own species name. These were all given in Latin, so anyone, anywhere in the world, can find and use the same names for exact identification. His name was really Karl von Linne, but like his system, it is always given in Latin, Linnaeus.

Where Did THAT Flower Come From?

Here are some of the best-known garden and wildflowers, and something of their history.

Amaryllis, the beautiful flower that springs up from a big bulb in an unbelievably short time, is a native of South America.

Anemones, those gaily colored spring flowers, grew wild in Palestine and the Levant. Some people think they were the original "lilies of the field" in the Bible.

During the Second Crusade, the Christian fleet brought back a ballast of good soil instead of the usual sand. This soil was spread out in Pisa, Italy—and anemones sprang up in the soil. The bulbs had come in as stowaways!

Bouncing Bet is a sweet-scented pretty little wildflower that grows along roadsides. It has been given many names—Pride of London, Lady-by-the-gate, Old Maid's Pink and Sweet Betty.

It was called Soapwort (wort means plant) by the early colonists. The women knew that the leaves and stems of this plant made a soap-like lather that would cleanse their silk and woolen clothes, and so they kept a patch of it growing near their cottage doors.

Begonias are natives from Bolivia.

Calendula, called Pot Marigold, grows wild and is native to areas from the Canary Islands to Persia.

Chrysanthemums all originated in China. They were cultivated there when Rome was new. They were brought to England in 1754.

Cockscombs, those spectacular red, yellow or white flowers that are well-named, came originally from India. They are very useful for making dry arrangements.

Cosmos, with delicate white, pink and rose-colored flowers and lacy foliage, came originally from Mexico.

Daffodils are real internationals. They were known by the Greeks and the Chinese in early days. They came to our country by way of the first colonists, who brought the bulbs with them so that they could have a touch of the old country in the new land.

Dahlias have a long history. Cortez found them being grown by the Aztecs when he invaded Mexico. He sent their seeds to Spain. From there they made their way up to Sweden, where they were grown by and named for the Swedish botanist, Andreas Dahl.

Delphiniums are natives of Siberia and Asia.

Flowering Quince, whose flowers come out in the early spring before its leaves are out, is a native of China. It was introduced to this country about a hundred and fifty years ago.

Geraniums, those wonderful house and windowbox flowers, are natives of South Africa. That is why they can stand so much heat and dryness. They were brought to England around 1700.

Gladiolas were wildflowers in South Africa. They were brought to England around 1800.

Hollyhocks originally came from China, but were found by the Crusaders in the Levant, who called them "the outlandish rose". They were brought to France, where they were called the "Holy Hock" because they had come from the Holy Land. When the Huguenots were persecuted and fled to England, they took hollyhock seed with them.

Iris are native to Central and Southern Europe and Northern Africa.

Jack-in-the-Pulpit is a native of North America. Its turnip-shaped root is very hot and acrid. Skunk cabbage and calla lilies are relatives. Every country child knows "Jack" in the spring, and its bunch of bright red berries in the fall.

Lilacs came from Constantinople to England in Queen Elizabeth's reign. Another species was found in Afghanistan, and the hybrid was bred in Rouen—hence "French lilacs".

Lily-of-the-Valley grows wild in Europe, Asia and Eastern North America.

Marigolds are native to Mexico. Like dahlias, their seed was sent back by the Spanish explorer, Cortez, and so the plant was called "Rose of the Indies". A large-size variety became naturalized along the North African coast, and from there it went to England. A smaller variety became naturalized in France. The Huguenots took its seed with them when they fled to England in 1573.

Nasturtiums grow wild in Chile and Peru. They were brought to Europe in the 16th century, and came to America by way of the early colonists.

Petunias are native to the southern part of South America.

Phlox is a native of the state of Pennsylvania.

Poppies first came from the area around Persia. They were found and cultivated by the early Egyptians.

Rhododendrons are natives of North America. They have a funny way of rolling their leaves up like cigars and pointing them downward when the temperature goes below freezing. This keeps the plant juices from evaporating in the cold.

Scarlet Sage comes from Brazil.

Snapdragons come from Southern Europe and the Mediterranean area. Press the flower at its sides between the fingers and watch the dragon open its mouth!

Sweet William, with its spicy fragrance, came first from China and Russia to the Pyrenees and then to England over three hundred years ago. The early colonists brought its seeds with them when they came to America.

Strawflowers, used so often in winter arrangements, are natives of Africa and Australia.

Tulips, natives of the Levant, were collected by the Turks, and were brought to Holland by merchant ships. They were raised in such quantities that in the 16th century they almost ruined the finances of that nation when the market for the bulbs collapsed.

Waterlilies are natives of tropical Africa. They were brought to Egypt by Egyptian armies fighting the Assyrians more than two thousand years ago.

Zinnias came from Mexico, like marigolds and dahlias. They found their way up to Germany, where they were named for a German professor of medicine, Johann Zinn, back in the 18th century. Luther Burbank in the United States is responsible for developing many new variations in the flower.

Weeds and Wildflowers

Chicory, with its bright blue flower is grown for its roots in France and Italy. The roots are ground up and used to blend with coffee. This type of coffee is popular in the southern part of the United States, especially in those states originally belonging to France.

Blue Bonnets, the State flower of Texas, have more than ninety species. See how many you can find if they are native to your area.

Goldenrod turns the fields and roadsides into a blaze of yellow in the late summer and fall in many sections of our country. Look at it carefully—there are more than a hundred and twenty-five different species of it. How many can you find and identify?

Jewelweed, often called *Touch-Me-Not,* is a strange plant. Put a bit of it in water, and see how the stem and leaves turn a silvery color. The leaves and stems, when crushed, will take away most of the sting of a bee, and it is said that the juice of this plant will heal poison ivy. Look for its small, ripe seedpods. Touch one lightly. Pop! Out will fly the seeds.

Milkweed, with its big pods filled with parachute-equipped seeds, is useful for craft projects. Its big flowerheads are the favorite of the monarch butterfly. Break a stem and see how the plant got its name.

Queen Anne's Lace, a weed in some places, is used in bridal bouquets in Trinidad. Look at a flower under the magnifying glass. That umbrel is made up of hundreds of tiny flowers. In the fall these flowerheads will curl up, and look like a small bird nest.

Solomon's Seal is a spring flower, with dainty little bells growing up a long, graceful stem. Its roots have scars that look like a seal—perhaps like Solomon's—who knows?

Violets are not always purple. There are more than a hundred domestic varieties. Violets all have five petals.

Flowers and Legends

Down through the years many stories and legends have grown up around flowers and how they were formed. Every country has its own favorites. These are only a very few:

Daisy. In Greek mythology, the god of spring saw a beautiful dryad dancing in the grass and fell in love with her. He ran to her, and tried to put his arms around her, but she was terrified of him. In pity, the gods transformed her into a small white flower so that she could escape him.

Dandelion. The Algonquin Indians have a pretty legend about the dandelion. One day the South Wind, who was a lazy fellow, was resting under a tree, dozing in the summer air. When he looked across the fields he saw a pretty, golden-haired girl. He thought she was very lovely, but he was too sleepy and lazy to go to her, or to call out to her.

Day after day during the summer he watched her, and admired

her, but did nothing to meet her. But one morning, near the end of summer, he looked across the prairie at her, and he was horrified. The young, golden-haired girl was gone. She had changed into a faded, white-haired, old woman. Then the South Wind knew that his brother, the North Wind, had touched the girl with his cold hands. When the South Wind went to her, the white hair blew off her head and she disappeared.

Every spring since that time, golden-haired girls appear in the fields and meadows and please the eyes of the South Wind until the North Wind withers them.

Forget-Me-Nots have a pretty little legend. One of the gods fell in love with a blue-eyed mortal, and she with him. He begged the gods to make the maiden immortal. They agreed—but on one condition. They said that when she had planted forget-me-nots all over the world they would grant her immortality.

She began the task, and every day he came to help her. Other mortals, seeing their love for each other, felt sorry for them and came to help them. And so forget-me-nots can be found all over the world, where the blue-eyed girl and her lover still work setting them out.

Lady's Thumb, a pretty little inconspicuous weed with a pinkish-red flower spike, is often found in clover fields. Its leaves usually look as though they had a brown splotch on them. Legend says that when Joseph cut his hand in his carpenter shop, Mary gathered some of the leaves of this plant and tried to make a poultice of them. They did not heal the cut, however, so Mary pinched the leaves. Ever since that time the plant has carried the mark of the Lady's thumb.

Lily-of-the-Valley has many legends. One, from England, tells how St. Leonard met a dragon and struggled with it for three days and three nights. On the fourth day he finally overcame the dragon, but he was severely wounded. Wherever a drop of his blood fell on the ground, a lily-of-the-valley sprang up so that pilgrims could follow in his footsteps. The legend says that if the pilgrims listen carefully, they can hear the tiny bells of the flower ringing out a song of victory.

The Passion Flower's strange shape has given it a religious significance. It is said that its ten petals represent the ten Apostles who were present at Christ's Crucifixion. The dark circle inside the petals represents the Crown of Thorns. The five central stamens are the five Wounds in His Hands, Feet and Side. The tendrils of the plant are the Scourges, and the finger-like leaves are the hands of the persecutors.

STATE FLOWERS

Which is YOUR state flower? All fifty of the states have chosen an official state flower, usually those most familiar to and best-loved by the people of the State. Here they are:

STATE	FLOWER	STATE	FLOWER
Alabama	Camellia	Montana	Sitterroot
Alaska	Forget-me-not	Nebraska	Goldenrod
Arizona	Saguaro	Nevada	Sagebrush
Arkansas	Apple Blossom	New Hampshire	Lilac
California	Poppy	New Jersey	Violet
Colorado	Columbine	New Mexico	Yucca
Connecticut	Mt. Laurel	New York	Wild Rose
Delaware	Peach Blossom	North Carolina	Dogwood
Florida	Orange Blossom	North Dakota	Wild Rose
Georgia	Cherokee Rose	Ohio	Carnation
Hawaii	Red Hibiscus	Oklahoma	Mistletoe
Idaho	Syringa	Oregon	Grape
Illinois	Violet	Pennsylvania	Mt. Laurel
Indiana	Peony	Rhode Island	Violet
Iowa	Wild Rose	South Carolina	Jessamine
Kansas	Sunflower	South Dakota	Pasque Flower
Kentucky	Goldenrod	Tennessee	Iris
Louisiana	Magnolia	Texas	Blue Bonnet
Maine	Pinecone	Utah	Sago Lily
Maryland	Blackeyed Susan	Vermont	Red Clover
Massachusetts	Arbutus	Virginia	Dogwood
Michigan	Apple Blossom	Washington	Rhododendron
Minnesota	Lady Slipper	West Virginia	Rhododendron
Mississippi	Magnolia	Wisconsin	Violet
Missouri	Hawthorn	Wyoming	Indian Paintbrush

Something To Make

Flowers and flowering plants can delight the eyes and please the nose. They can also be used in developing manual creative skills from making a simple daisy chain or flower lei up to other skills, including cooking. The emphasis should be placed upon the *materials,* however, not the finished product. Identification, conservation, exploration and appreciation are all important products in learning about flowers.

Flower Necklaces

Children love to make and to wear them. The very easiest is the daisy chain—something that can be made while sitting down, perhaps telling a story. Each person merely picks a daisy with a stem about two inches long and slits the stem up near the flower with his fingernail or a sharp-pointed stick. Pick another daisy, poke the stem of that one through the slit, then pull the daisy up toward the first one. Then slit the second stem, and keep on in this way until the daisy chain is long enough to go over the head. In no time at all, everyone can have a necklace, and a daisy crown to match.

A *lei* is a bit more involved. To make one that will last for some party or special occasion, pick lots of daisies, marigolds, chrysanthemums, zinnias or other flowers with flat, round heads. Put the flowers in water for several hours so that they can "harden off", and will stay nice and fresh. Then one by one, cut off the flower-heads and with a long needle and thread string them, pushing each flower up against the one above it. Continue until the lei is long enough to go over the head easily. Then tie the ends of the thread, and there you are! The lei will keep nice and fresh until you are ready to use it if you will put it in a plastic bag, and keep it in the refrigerator. Nice for a special award for Dad, or for Sis' birthday, or to welcome Grandpa and Grandma.

Flower Pictures

This project combines several elements—finding the material to be used, collecting it (nothing on the conservation list), bringing it home and drying it.

To dry, select flowers or plants that have flat heads, like Queen Anne's lace, daisies, or pansies, plus some of the pretty, graceful grasses and ferns. Spread them out carefully on paper toweling, cover with another layer of toweling, then with a heavy weight, such as a big-city telephone book, or a pile of magazines. Let them dry out thoroughly. It may be several weeks until they are flat and dry.

Then buy an inexpensive glassed frame at the five-and-dime. Cut a piece of blotting paper just the right size and color. Look over the dried materials, and then lay some of them out on the blotting paper in a pleasing, graceful design. When the design is just right, lift up each piece, add a tiny bit of glue to its back, and put it back again into its place. Then put the flower picture into the frame— and stand back to admire it. These pictures can be used for very nice gifts.

Instead of the bought frame, try making some of these flower and plant pictures on slabs of wood, or on pieces of flat driftwood. The color of the wood will blend beautifully with the arrangement. Spray it afterwards with a clear plastic spray, and put the wooden picture upon a little easel, or a plaque-stand from a shop that sells oriental objects.

Growing Things

Children enjoy planting and watching things grow—especially if the thing grows rapidly. Bulbs provide a pleasant way to both plant and watch.

100

Fall Blooming. Buy the bulbs of several Autumn Crocuses (they really are not crocuses!), and watch a miracle. Place the bulbs in a low vase or saucer on a windowsill. They will grow without soil or water! They will bloom, too! Those bulbs had the flowers all tucked inside, all ready to come out.

When the bulbs have finished blooming, you can set them out in the garden. In the spring they will make foliage and seedpods. When the foliage has died, usually in June, the bulbs can be lifted and saved for another autumn miracle.

Spring Blossoms. Children enjoy seeing the rapid growth and the blooming of spring bulbs indoors. Paperwhite Narcissus is among the fastest and prettiest. Buy several bulbs. Place pebbles or fish-bowl chips in a low bowl, and put the bulbs in among them so that they stand up straight and sturdy. Add enough water to cover the bottoms of the bulbs. Keep the bowl in a cool, dark place until you see some signs of growth, then bring the bowl out into the sunlight. Growth will be rapid, and before you know it the bulbs will flower. Don't try to save the bulbs for re-planting. They have been forced, and won't do well again.

The Amaryllis is one of the most spectacular to plant and watch. A bulb, compared to some of the others, will seem expensive, but it will be well worthwhile to buy a first-grade bulb. It will produce a most beautiful plant, and really spectacular flowers—and do it remarkably rapidly.

Plant the bulb in a pot that *almost* fits it. It likes to be crowded. Use good soil, and place the bulb so that only the bottom third is covered with soil. It should look like a sitting duck in the pot. Water, and place in a cool, dark place until you see signs of growth. Then bring it out into the light, and it will grow so fast that you can almost *see* it! Up and up will come a long, strong stem, then flower-buds, and finally one or more—usually more—perfectly gorgeous flowers that will bring pleasure for quite a long time.

When the flowers have all faded, cut off the flower stalk and feed the plant with some plant food. It must make food for next year's bloom. Finally, when the leaves have died, the bulb can be stored in a cool, dry, dark place until next year.

Drying Flowers

There are two chief methods, the old and the new. The old way simply involves hanging certain types of flowers that dry well up-side down in a dark, airy place. Strawflowers, grasses, statice, baby's breath and cockscomb are favorite flowers for this method.

In most cases, the flowers should be picked in the late morning, after the dew has evaporated. The cockscomb, however, should be picked while wet with dew and then placed, spikes up, in a vase or bucket for three days (no water). Then they should be hung upside down until thoroughly dry.

The second method is newer. It involves using a moisture absorbing material called silica gel that goes under several trade names. In this method flowers are cut from their stems and attached to florist wire. They are then buried in the silica gel mixture for several days, usually from two to eight. They come out looking fresh, not dry-looking, and can be worked into very lovely flower arrangements that are permanent. Directions vary with the flower or plant material used, so read the directions carefully.

The gel will seem expensive, but it can be used over and over again and can be the means of starting you on a new and very interesting hobby.

Flower Arranging

This need not be an esoteric art that only the highly trained can enjoy. Children love to pick and arrange flowers and can make surprisingly beautiful and interesting arrangements with just a bit of advice and help.

First, encourage originality. A few flowers in an unusual container can be more interesting than a big bunch of flowers crowded into a vase. Encourage the child to see the possibilities of using a shell, or a basket, a mug, a bottle, a small pitcher—anything that seems to suit the flowers to be used.

Next, be sure that the child uses enough water (lots of people never fill a container, and the poor flowers die of thirst very quickly). If the flowers won't stay in place, show the child how to use the various types of holders, such as needles, rolled up chickenwire, frogs, and the like.

Then encourage him to think of the *design* that will look best. He should think of the shape that will go nicely with the container, and arrange the flowers so that they will fit that shape. Perhaps it is a circle, or a triangle, or an L-shape.

To get the right effect for the shape selected, large flowers should go near the center, smaller ones along the outside.

There's a rule of thumb that says that the highest point of a flower arrangement should be one-half to two times the height of a tall vase, and one and a half times the width of a low vase or dish, whichever is used for the container.

Children will feel important and useful when they are given the job of providing the flower arrangement for the dining room table, or for a special occasion such as a birthday party or holiday. Don't wait for special occasions, however. Everyday-beauty is important, too.

If you belong to a garden club, see whether it can't sponsor a

102

junior showing of flower arrangements. It wil provide a new incentive for the child, and give status to the project.

Miniature Arrangements

These can be real charmers. First, assemble some tiny containers—perhaps a little perfume bottle, a babyfood jar, a screwtop from a glass jar, or the tops of empty deodorant bottles. These last are often pretty fluted shapes, and are deep and wide enough to make charming miniature containers. Little foil containers also work out nicely.

Fill these tiny containers with Oasis, the material you can buy at a florist shop. Soak the Oasis thoroughly in water before you cut out tiny dabs of it to fit the containers. It will hold water nicely, but it takes time to absorb it. When all the containers have been filled with wet Oasis, you're ready to start arranging.

Find and collect some tiny plants and flowers—very small daisies, or violets, or small pansies, or other pretties. Bring them in, and very carefully insert their little stems into the Oasis. If the stems are too weak to poke through it, make a small hole in the Oasis with a toothpick, and put the little stem into the hole. If you like, add a tiny bit of moss around the top to hide the Oasis.

These make charming banquet or place settings, and for a breakfast or convalescent's tray. Also, use them as May baskets for the children to give their friends and neighbors.

Flower Coasters

Cut circles out of heavy cardboard, cork, or other material. The rim of a coffee cup makes a good tracing guide. These circles will be the coasters.

They may be decorated in a number of ways. If the cardboard is white, a flower design can be cut out of paper (colorful ads are often very pretty), and glued on. Or the design can be painted or crayoned directly to the base. Or make a stencil from stiff paper by drawing the design, cutting it out and placing the cutout over the coaster, then painting or crayoning within the stencil.

Whatever the method used, the coasters should have several coats of clear shellac to make them waterproof. If they are to be used just once, for some special occasion, it will not be necessary to shellac them.

Salt-and-Flour Flowers

This is a formula and directions for a sort of modeling material that can be used to make small objects, such as flowers, beads, small animals, and other articles. It takes:

4 tablespoons of table salt

Flower Coaster   Garden Bug   Butterfly

6 tablespoons of flour
3 tablespoons of water

Make a smooth paste of the flour and water. Stir the salt in a pan over low heat until it crackles. Then mix it into the flour and water mixture, and knead it like dough until it is nice and smooth. Pack in a jar with a tight cover until you are ready to use it.

Take small amounts of it in the hands and model it into the shape of flowers, birds, butterflies, animals, or other small objects. Place the articles on a piece of wax paper and let them dry out thoroughly. Paint them with watercolors, tempera, ink or dye. For a finished look, give them a coating of varnish or clear nail polish.

If making flowers, you can insert some lengths of wires into the model while it is moist and let it dry as above.

To make pretty beads, roll a small amount of the modeling clay between the palms of the hand. Then use a cuticle stick or toothpick to work a small design into it, such as lines for petals. Use a large pin to make a hole through each bead for stringing. Let the beads dry thoroughly, then paint as above and string. Pretty!

Garden Bugs

Look at some bugs, beetles and insects. Really *look* at them. Observe their shape, size, and the colorful designs on their bodies—stripes, polka dots, all sorts of designs!

Then make some Bottle Cap Bugs just for fun. Collect some bottle caps from soft drink bottles. Trace the bottle cap shape on a circle of white paper, or colored paper, and crayon the bug's design on it. Cut out carefully.

Take a hammer and a nail and make a hole in the cap, off-center. Bend wires or pipecleaners and push the ends through the hole. Leave a loop of the wire for the head of the bug, then spread out the ends for legs. How many legs should it have? Look and see— then use enough wire to make the right number of legs. Now glue the circle of paper onto the bottle cap.

Try making some "bugs" out of screw-on tops. Take out the cork or plastic liner, place the wires or strips of paper or other "leg" material across the cap, then push the liner back in, to hold the legs in place. Paint the cap in a bug's colors and design.

Butterflies

Watch for butterflies, and note the colors and designs on their wings. Take crayons and try to sketch them.

Cut butterfly shapes out of tissue paper, and crayon the colors of the real butterfly's wings. Stick a pin through the paper, then into the eraser of a pencil. There! A very natural-looking butterfly.

Or crumple a piece of plastic wrap and wire a body around it with a pipecleaner or bit of copper wire. Put a border of colored, gummed paper around the wings.

Or use the hinged type of clothespin for the body, plastic wrap or tissue paper for the wings. Decorate it. Hang all of these by strings from a doorway, or other place where they can "hover", and seem to fly in the breeze.

Flower Masks

Everybody can make his own. Needed—a large piece of cardboard. The piece that comes from the laundry in men's shirts is a good size. Draw a BIG flower on the cardboard and color it with crayons, or paint it with tempera or poster paint. Any flower will do—a daisy, tulip, rose, aster, chrysanthemum.

Attach an eight-inch stick to the lower half of the flower so that the mask can be held up in front of the face. Then, very carefully, cut out two small holes to look through. Then play with the masks. Make up a flower story.

Or, omit the holes, and use the masks for fans on a hot day.

Or, attach the flower drawings to sticks about a yard long, and use them for garden markers or lawn decorations, or to mark the edges of the driveway.

Clover Honey

Children love to collect the ingredients for this and watch it being made. They also love to eat it afterwards! They must look for and collect the following:

40 red clover blossoms
60 white, low-growing clover blossoms (Include some sweet clover, too, if it is available)
Petals from two, medium-size roses

Then, take five pounds of white sugar, add just enough water to moisten, and bring it to a boil for two minutes. Put it on the back of the stove to cool.

Add the clover blossoms and rose petals while the mixture is still hot, and let the whole thing stand for an hour or more. Then strain, and put the syrup into a jar. It will make about a quart of "honey", very good on pancakes or waffles. Cut the recipe in half if a pint of honey will be enough.

Rose Potpourri

Down through the ages there have been many recipes developed for rose potpourri, but many of them call for ingredients that are not only expensive but are also hard to find. Many of them take a great deal of time and are very complicated. This is one of the simplest, yet it makes very fragrant sachet or potpourri.

It may be stored in glass or china jars or bowls, or put into small net bags for use in closets and bureau drawers. The scent will last a long time, and a pint or pound will fill several jars and bags.

First, pick the roses late in the morning after the dew has evaporated. Tear the petals off the roses one by one, until you have about a quart of them. Then put a piece of cheesecloth over an old window screen, and set it in a shady, dry place where the air can circulate over and under the petals on the screen. In spreading the petals, try to keep them separated as much as possible. Riffle them from time to time so that they will dry evenly. They will get like tissue paper, but they won't crumble.

Dry the petals of larkspur, calendula and other flowers separately if you'd like to add a bit of color to the mixture. Or add the leaves of sweet-scented plants like verbena, geranium, or sweet-scented herbs. Keep all of these separate from the rose petals, and add them in small quantities after they are all perfectly dry.

The recipe for the Rose Potpourri is not difficult:

6 cups of dried petals
½ teaspoon of ground cloves
½ teaspoon of cinnamon
½ teaspoon of allspice
½ teaspoon of mint flakes
1½ teaspoons of ground orris root (Buy it at a drugstore. It acts as a fixative for the potpourri.)

Add the spices to the dried petals. Sift in the ground orris root. Mix them well in a big bowl, then pack them into covered pottery or glass jars or bowls, or into little net bags. The bags can be squares of net, caught up at the corners and tied with a pretty ribbon. Store the net bags in a plastic bag until you are ready to use them or to give them away.

Keep a bowl or jar of the potpourri in a room, and occasionally take the lid off, letting the rose perfume pervade the room.

PART VI

Crafts From
Nature's Waterfront

Something To Look For

Beaches, whether fresh or salt water, may give a first impression of
being nothing but sun, surf and sand. Look again! Look closely and
leisurely, and a whole new world of animal and plant life will
show up.

Look for what the waves bring in. Look for driftwood, sometimes
worm-eaten boards, sometimes the trunks and roots of trees. Look
at the pebbles, worn so smooth by the pounding of the waves. On
some beaches, look for pebbles of semi-precious stones washed up
along the shore.

Look for shells. Some are so small that they look like grains of
sand. Some are so large that they may be used for planters, or for
making a shell trumpet, or ramekins at a sea-food dinner. Look at
the delicate shapes, the graceful designs, the soft colors of shells.

Look for sand dollars, those strange-looking finds with a big star
in their center.

Watch the seabirds—the gulls swooping and screaming, the little
wading birds skimming along the water's edge.

Look for sails along the horizon, and think of the olden days of
the sea clippers with their billowing sails. Look at the clouds racing
across the sky. Look at the wonderful sunsets over the water, and
the moonpath at night. Look at the swirly patterns on the sand
when the tide goes out. Look at the dunes, like miniature moun-
tains. Look at the small plants that hold these dunes in place and
prevent them from changing their forms and locations as the wind
blows them.

Look for seaweeds. They may be coral-encrusted in warm waters.
Sometimes they may be the very dark species that grow at great

depths, and have been uprooted by some great storm.

Look for little seapools, where sea-creatures may be marooned, or be living together. Look for clams hiding in the sand, or for footprints along the tide line. Smell the salt air. Build sand castles, and watch the waves demolish them.

Look for strange objects that the tides may bring in. Sometimes the pretty glass balls used to buoy nets will wash in from great distances away. Sometimes sun-faded bottles, or bits of boxes, or children's toys—almost anything, at some time or other, may show up.

Go out soon after a storm and look for what may have been washed up—seaweed from dark ocean-bottoms, shells you never saw before, all sorts of flotsam and jetsam.

Look for the beach treasures—things that are especially beautiful, rare, or interesting and start a collection. Think up ways of using them in crafts, so that the beach holidays will be remembered.

Something To Talk About

How *sand* is made. The different kinds of sand, some soft as silk, some coarse as sandpaper, some white, some pink, some black, some grey. Talk about the action of the waves upon the shore. Look for signs of beach erosion. Notice the tide line. Is the sand finer or coarser there? Perhaps it is a pebble beach. Talk about how those pebbles got so smooth and rounded.

Talk about *shells,* the great family called Mollusca or Mollusks. Some of the mollusks have only one shell, and so are called univalves. Many of these have the lovely coiled, snail-shaped shells, and belong to the big snail family that has more than 30,000 members—a very big family indeed.

Many of the shells on the beach will be bivalves, those with two shells hinged together with a tough membrane. These are the types that we enjoy as seafood—the clams, oysters, scallops and mussels. Look for the thinnish, bluish-black shells of the *mussels,* often very easy to find on the beach. Talk about how the shells are joined together by what looks like a hinge. Find and talk about *scallops—* the pretty, scalloped, ridged shells that come in all sorts of pretty colors. We eat the *muscle* of the scallop. This muscle opens and shuts the shell, and propels it zigzagging through the water.

Talk about the little *cockle shells.* Cockles have a long "foot" that lets them jump several inches. Some are edible. Remember the song, "Cockles and mussels alive, alive-o".

Talk about *clams.* The Indians made their "wampum", or shell money, out of the quahog clamshells. Baby quahogs are the "cherrystone" and "littleneck" clams on the menus of restaurants.

Talk about that strange-looking shell with a hole right in the middle. It is a *keyhole limpet.* Limpets have very strong feet and attach themselves to rocky shores, or to seaweed.

Talk about that weird little creature that looks like a miniature armored tank. It is a *chiton,* and it *is* armored. It has eight overlapping plates held together by a strong mantle called the "girdle". Chitons live on rocks at the shore and eat algae.

Shells are often named for the way they look—Tulip Shell, Olive Shell, Turk's Cap, Fig, Venus' Comb, Scotch Bonnet, Slipper Shell, Cup-and-Saucer.

If you are lucky, you may find a shining, china-like lovely shell. It is probably a cowrie—and people have collected, admired, and even worn them as jewelry for hundreds of years.

Don't reject broken shells. Sometimes some of these fragments are so colored and shaped that they can be used to make lovely shell pictures and plaques. Collect them, and also look for and collect thin, interesting shapes of driftwood on which your shell pictures can be mounted.

Talk about *crustaceans*—the crabs, lobsters and shrimp. Visit a fishing boat when it comes in with its catch. Or visit a local fish market, and take time to look over the many kinds of fish—bass, catfish, cod, mackerel, swordfish, perch, red snapper, trout, tuna. Some are saltwater fish, others freshwater. Some are large enough to be cut into steaks, others so small they can be eaten in one bite. How many can you identify by sight? Talk about their fins and tails, and how they help the fish to glide through the water. We have copied fish when we use flippers on our feet when swimming. Notice the colors of fish, and the designs of color on their scales. Make a fish print (directions in this Part).

Talk about *driftwood.* Where do you suppose that thin, curved, worm-eaten piece came from originally? What was that board once a part of? Where did that tree trunk and those roots once grow? Talk about its color—sometimes grey, sometimes almost white where it has been bleached by the sun and salt water. Look at the marks of the waves on it, those beautiful curved lines that seem to make a design. Talk about the colors it gives to flames when it is burned. The salt and other sea minerals give it this magic. Save interesting pieces for craft projects. Collect small pieces for gifts to friends with fireplaces.

Talk about *plant life* along the shore. Why are the trees all bent in one direction? What is the prevailing wind? Why are the trees and shrubs all rather low in size? Talk about the little vines, grasses and other plants that keep the sand from "walking away". Why do beach-owners and public agencies try so hard to *plant* the dunes?

Talk about *bayberry,* if it grows in your area. Try to find some with grey berries on it. Feel how sticky and waxy they are. Our early colonists used these waxy berries to make the first bayberry candles—and they are still being made and bought for their pretty, soft color and their fragrant smell.

Talk about *cranberries*, if they grow anywhere nearby. The Indians showed the early colonists how to cook and dry them. Cranberries were very probably on the menu of the very first Thanksgiving dinner.

Talk about the *sea* (or lake, bay or other body of water). How salty is the water? Find out in this Part. What other shores does that body of water touch? Look at a map and find out.

Talk about the *Coast Guard*, the *Weather Bureau*, the *lighthouse*, the *buoys* that mark the channels. Talk about the great sea routes, and the part they have played in civilization. Talk about the *underwater world*. Go snorkling or scuba diving and visit this world.

Visit the public library and look up books about shells, fish, seaweed, and other marine life. Learn and talk about the names for plant and animal life in the sea and along the shores.

Something To Make

Beaches, whether freshwater or saltwater, provide an almost prodigal supply of things that can be made into interesting craft projects. Everyone enjoys roaming along the beach, looking for shells, driftwood, colored pebbles, starfish, limpets, sea dollars, rocks, seaweed, and other debris not found anywhere else. These craft treasures may have to be left behind when the holiday is over and the family returns inland. But when the sea-treasures are made into craft articles, they remain as a constant reminder of pleasant, sunny days at the beach and the wonders of the shores and sea.

Shell Crafts

Shells have all sorts of craft uses. Big ones make very pretty dishes for miniature gardens, or as adjuncts for flower arrangements, or as dishes for seafood meals.

Use small ones for Christmas tree decorations. Just glue a gold string to one end, and leave enough length of string for tying the shell to the tree. Tiny shells can be grouped into a pretty little cluster, and also used for the tree. Small shells, on a string knotted between each shell, make a pretty necklace. String them on a piece of narrow, round elastic for a matching bracelet.

Shells of all sizes and shapes, whole and broken, can be combined into beautiful shell pictures or plaques.

Seashell Trumpet. Remember the book, *The Lord of the Flies?* You may not be able to find a shell like the one in the book, but

HORN SHELL

OLIVE SHELL

BUTTERFLY

NUT CLAM

Shell Creature

any large shell can be made into a trumpet. Find the shell, bore a hole in the side of it, or cut off the apex. Blow hard into either of these openings, and a deep, loud tone will come out of it.

Pebble-Shell Animals. A nice way to combine pebbles and shells. Collect a supply of pebbles and shells in various sizes and shapes, but keep them on the small side. Look over the pebbles. Does any of them remind you vaguely of the shape of some animal? Use the shells for ears, legs, paws, or other parts of the animal. Glue them on with a heavy-duty glue, such as Sobo, Elmer's, Nu-Glu or other trade name. It will take patience to hold them in place while the glue hardens. Sometimes a wisp of cotton glued to the shell and then glued to the pebble will stick better than the shell-to-stone.

Shell Creatures. Everyone has seen animals and birds made by combining various kinds and sizes of shells and glueing them together. This Penguin was made of a horn shell, olive shell, butterfly shell and nut clam shell. Its head is the horn shell, its body the olive shell, its base the nut clam shell, and its feet the little butterfly shells. The wing sections are painted on with black enamel. Try the wisp-of-cotton technique mentioned above if you have any trouble making the shells stick together.

Shell Plaques. These can be so simple that a very young child can make them. Perhaps just a simple flower, worked out in shells with a bit of seaweed or drift wood added. They can also be works of art, so beautifully designed and executed that they *must* be mounted and framed, or used as plaques on little stands. No exact design can be described because the materials collected, their shapes and colors, will more or less dictate the design. It is important to collect a good supply of shells, pebbles, stones, crystals, seaweed, and other bits of beach life so that you can have a wide choice of shapes, sizes and colors. Look especially for broken pieces of large shells. They will provide unusual curves, flat bits, coils, and many odd shapes that combine well with the smaller, unbroken shells.

To make an interesting plaque, use a hot-plate tile for the background and paint it a flat, dark color so that the delicate shades of the shells will be in contrast. Then arrange the shells, pieces of shells, pebbles, and other material you plan to use. Experiment with the layout until you find an arrangement that looks right. It may be that certain broken shells fit together to suggest calla lilies

111

or other flowers. You can't tell until you work at it. But try to use the material so that everything blends in color and forms a design pleasing to the eye. Don't rush this part of the project. It is a bit like a jigsaw puzzle. At first there is a lot of hunting and fitting—then suddenly the picture begins to emerge.

When you are proud of the design you have created, glue the shells into place, one by one, using a heavy-duty glue such as Sobo, Elmer's, Nu-Glu or other. This will also take time and patience. Let the design sit until the glue has hardened, and the shells are securely in place.

Mount the tile—or have an expert mount it—with a background of burlap in a shadow frame, and hang it with pride. A pair of these on a wall are very decorative.

Use the same technique to make charming plaques for the home or for gifts by using pieces of driftwood as background, instead of the more formal tile. Try to find flat, thin driftwood with watermarks on it, and with the soft, bleached surface that will contrast beautifully with the soft colors of the shells and pebbles, etc. If the wood is worm-eaten, so much the better. Use the designs of the sand and water on the wood as part of the total arrangement. Glue a cord or hook on the back for hanging, or better still, buy several of those little plate or statue holders, easel-like, that often can be found in shops that sell oriental objects..

Shell Bag or Shopping Bag. These are very popular for summer use—and very expensive when bought in a store. The untrimmed bags, however, are inexpensive, so decorate your own. They are not difficult to make. Even Sis can make a small one for herself.

Buy a plain, undecorated straw bag or shopping bag in a pleasing size and shape. Then decorate it with shells, pebbles, seaweed, starfish, and other marine objects.

Collect shells of as many different sizes, shapes and colors as possible. Include those pretty fragments of large, broken shells. Often the colors in them are deeper than many of the smaller shells. Wash all the shells thoroughly, dry them, and buff them with a soft cloth.

Then lay the shells on a sheet of paper about the size of the area of the bag to be decorated—usually a fairly large design in one corner, drifting off to a smaller one in the other corner. The design shouldn't look too heavy. Arrange the shells, seaweed, pebbles and other material until the design is graceful and pleasing. Take your time. The design is very important. The better the design, the more beautiful the bag will be.

Then, one by one, transfer the material to the bag, glueing each piece into place. Small, flat shells can be glued easily directly to the bag. The larger shells, and the broken pieces, sometimes quite long

112

and narrow, are a bit harder to glue and will require patience. The wisp-of-cotton technique may very well be necessary for the larger, heavy material, especially the larger, whole shells.

Glue a wisp of cotton (not the medical kind) to the bag where the shell is to go. Then put some glue in the shell, stuff the shell with cotton, and put some glue on the cotton that shows. Add a bit of glue to the cotton on the bag, then put the two bits of cotton together, press down, and hold until the glue is set. It is surprising how well this technique works, even with quite large shells.

When the design is glued in place, look it over carefully. Does it need a few more small shells sprinkled around, or leading into the smaller design? Does it need a sprig of coraled seaweed to give height to the design? Don't overdo, but now is the time to make the design as dramatic as possible.

Then let it all dry thoroughly. Spray with a clear plastic coating for added strength and shine.

Snow Storm

Such a nice project for a hot day, and such a nice gift to make for Christmas!

Find a small, round, screwtop jar. Sometimes jams and jellies come in them. Paint the *outside* of the screwtop lid any color you like. Red, green, or gold will look very pretty for a Christmas gift. The *inside* of this screwtop will be the base for the snow scene.

Collect a variety of small, pretty pebbles, bits of quartz, small shells and such. Add a tiny figurine of a bird, fish, small animal, or little figure, if you like. Use waterproof cement, and glue your little scene into place inside the screwtop, making it as pretty and as interesting as possible. Then let the design dry out thoroughly.

Fill the jar full of water, and add two tablespoons of mothflakes or mica snow. Then screw the lid onto the jar and invert so that the lid becomes the base—and there's a violent snowstorm settling down over the little scene. Very gay, and no one passing by can refrain from inverting it, to work up a storm!

Seal the lid with cement or with paraffin, so that the jar won't leak.

Rock Sand

Make your own! Collect a supply of small rocks, preferably those with rough sides. Crush them with a hammer. Keep the colors separate—they're a way of identifying the kind of rock. For example, black or dark red sand is usually basalt. Shiny white sand is quartz. Dull white is often limestone. Rocks making more than one color sand are usually granite. Use the sand you have made for Sand Painting, described in this Part.

Rock Bookends

Look for and collect two interesting rocks, large enough to hold books in place. For each of the bookends, cut a wax or plastic milk carton in half. Then cut the bottom half diagonally to use as a mold. Tilt it so that the open side is up, and fill it with plaster of paris (see instructions for mixing in Tools & Equipment). Then insert the rock into the plaster of paris in such a way that its prettiest side is showing. Let the plaster dry, remove the carton, smooth the edges of the plaster, and glue a piece of felt or cork on the bottom so the bookends won't scratch the furniture. A spray of clear plastic will give a "wet" look to the rocks. Very useful and effective.

Animal-Print Paperweight

A nice way to use a smooth, handsome stone and learn the shapes of animal footprints too!

Find and collect several smooth stones the right size and weight to use as paperweights. Try to find some that sit without rolling. Try to find them with varying shapes, too.

Paint these stones with enamel—white makes a good background color if you want to paint the footprints black, but use the colors that will fit into the decor of the room in which they will be used.

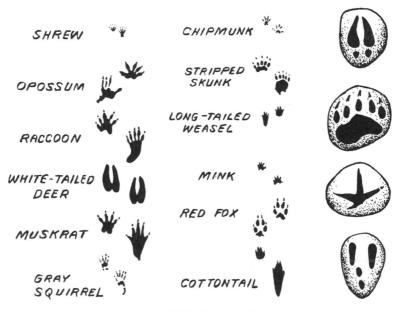

Animal Print Paperweight

114

Of course, if the stones are a very pretty color without painting, you can use them "as is".

Glue a piece of felt on the base so the paperweights won't scratch the table or desk. Then very carefully, with charcoal or a pencil, sketch the footprint of the animal you want to use. When the sketch is all finished on the stone, look at it, and see if it is just the way you want it. Then *paint* it, using a color contrasting to the color of the stone. One of these makes a nice paperweight for Dad's desk. A row of them, each with the print of a different animal, makes a nice decoration for a child's room, or a hunter's den.

Stone Paintings

These are similar to the Animal-Print Paperweights, but use a different design. Again, collect smooth, interesting stones, the right size and shape for paperweights. Paint them with a white or other color enamel. Glue a piece of felt on the base to prevent furniture scratches.

Then sketch some sort of scene or object onto the rock. It might be an abstract design. It might be a marine scene. One made in Italy has a white background with a sketch of an octopus holding a starfish. Sketches of lobsters, sea anemones, fish, coral, or other marine items make nice mementos of a beach holiday.

For a gardener, the rock could be decorated with a flower or bunch of flowers. For a bird-lover, a seagull or other bird. For a desert dweller, cactus or other desert life. For a sportsman, some type of sports equipment. For Dad, a big V I P for a Very Important Person.

Stone House

A nice beach project, and one that children enjoy doing. They must collect a good supply of pebbles, all about an inch in diameter and length. Cut a base for the house out of heavy cardboard about six inches square, or four by six inches if the house is to be rectangular. The size doesn't have to be exact. Don't make it too big, however, because it will be too heavy. The base can be a tile, a shingle, or a piece of wood—driftwood, perhaps. Mark off an inch all around the base as a guide for putting up the pebble walls of the house.

The first row of pebbles should be glued, one by one, onto the edge of the base, leaving space for a doorway. Use heavy-duty glue —Sobo, Elmer's, NuGlu or such—and let each pebble set before putting a pebble on top of it. Then glue the next row of pebbles onto the first row, and so on, until the house is the right height. Leave openings for windows, if you like.

Add a roof made by bending a piece of cardboard in the middle to make a peak. Try different shapes of roofs—a nearly flat roof

Pebble People

for a modern house, a gable roof, or a very steep roof for a house like the witch's in *Hansel and Gretel*. Cover the roof with bark shingles, starting at the bottom of the roof and working up so that each shingle overlaps another.

Use triangles of cardboard to make the end gables. Leave flaps that will fit in between the roof and the walls. Add a chimney if you like. Lay out a yard, and make a stone path leading to the house.

Pebble Star Map

Collect various sizes of pebbles, from large to small. Observe the various constellations in the evening sky, and next day, on the beach or in the yard, arrange the pebbles in the outlines of the various constellations. Use a star book for reference, if necessary. Then learn the names of the constellations so that you can identify them quickly in the sky.

Pebble People

When made with care and imagination, Pebble People can be very clever and amusing decorations.

Collect two small, flat pebbles for feet, one larger flat pebble for the body, and one flat but slightly thicker pebble for the head of this Pebble Person. Paint lines to indicate the eyes and mouth.

Glue strands of wool yarn flat, back from the forehead, and over the top of the head. Braid the hair into two or two-and-a-half inch braid. Spray the whole thing, yarn hair and all, with clear lacquer, and smooth the hair down flat before the lacquer dries. This Pebble Girl is a gay little thing. Create a family for her.

Stone Jewelry

Find stones or smooth pebbles that are well-shaped and have a nice color. Give them a coating of clear lacquer or varnish if they have not been "tumbled" to make them shiny and smooth.

Use sixteen- or eighteen-gage copper wire to make a cage to hold the stone, and to hang them on a chain or cord as a pendant. Wind

116

the copper wire around the stone just enough to hold it securely, but not to cover very much of it from sight. Use pliers to pull the wire tight, and to secure it by winding its ends securely. Work the wire into a loop for hanging the stone.

Should you get expert at this, and enjoy your results, you can use silver wire, but it is very expensive in comparison.

Small stones may also be glued to bits of polished wood, or driftwood, or to jewelry "findings" for pins and earrings. Or try glueing small, pretty stones to squares, circles, or other shapes of leather. Punch holes in the scraps of leather, and string them into a necklace or a belt.

Smoothing Pebbles

The best method is to "tumble" them in a tumbler, some of which are relatively inexpensive. For an interesting home project, however, and for use with a small supply of irregularly shaped rocks, you can improvise a tumbler. Fill a coffee can about a third full of the rough pebbles that you think will shine up nicely. Then fill the can with water, put the top on securely, and place it where everyone passes it. Each time anyone goes by, he or she should give the can as many shakes as possible. Do this for several weeks. If shaken often enough, the pebbles will be rubbed shiny-smooth.

Rock Mosaic

Go on a rock hunt and bring back a good supply of small pebbles in as many different shapes and colors as possible. Wash them all carefully and dry them. Decide upon a design—perhaps a beach scene, or a desert scene. Draw it on a piece of heavy cardboard, or a shingle, or piece of driftwood.

Then, using the various rocks, fill in the design, taking the shapes, sizes and colors of the stones into account. Use a fast-drying, heavy-duty glue. When the mosaic is thoroughly dry, spray it with a clear lacquer or varnish to give the stones a shine, or the "wet" look. Very effective.

Waterscope

A big help in looking into pools to see what sealife is below the surface. Find a five-gallon tin can. Cut out most of the bottom, but leave an inch-wide rim. Get your local hardware man to cut a piece of glass for you to fit over the hole and rest firmly on the inch-wide rim. Insulate the glass with putty or warm tar so that water will not leak through.

Then submerge the bucket about three-fourths of its height, bend over it, and peer into the pool. You may find a new shell, or a piece of unusual seaweed, or other interesting marine life.

Sand Tracks

Making footprints in the sand is fun—and it will be fun to preserve those footprints. They make good souvenirs of a trip to the beach.

First, get Baby Brother or other member of the family to walk across firm, wet sand, and select one of the footprints to preserve. Then work fast.

Put a cardboard collar around the print, not touching it anywhere, or disturbing it. The collar should be about three or four inches wide, and long enough to overlap when sunk in the sand around the print.

Prepare plaster of paris as directed under Tools and Equipment in this book. Pour the plaster gently into the cardboard circle so that the footprint is entirely covered, and about an inch deep. Add a hook made out of a paper clip if you plan to hang the plaster cast.

Let the cast "set" for about an hour. Then pull out the cardboard collar, and wash the cast to remove any sand. Brush it with an old toothbrush if necessary.

Better make several casts of Baby Brother's footprint. Grandparents will want one.

Try making casts of handprints, too. And get the family cat or dog to walk across wet sand and make *its* prints!

Sand Painting

This is an American Indian art form. Children enjoy it. Use sand from lake or ocean beach. Sift it to remove any larger pebbles, twigs or other debris.

Color or dye the sand. Decide upon what colors you will need. Fill a glass jar half full of sand, and drop in several drops of liquid coloring. Screw the top on tight, and shake the sand until all of it is dyed. Remember that damp sand will look darker than when it dries. Then spread that sand out and let it dry completely before using. Do this for every color you use.

Sketch the picture—abstract, landscape, seascape, flower picture, sports scene of whatever you want—on a large sheet of cardboard. Then cover the various sections of the scene, one at a time as you work, with white glue spread on with a paintbrush. The glue may be diluted with water, and often a second coat of glue helps to retain the sand better. As each section is covered with glue, sprinkle it with the proper shade of sand. Then hold the picture over a sheet of paper and carefully shake off the excess sand. Pour it back into its bottle. Do this for all the colored sections of the scene. A second coating of glue and sand may improve textures in some areas.

A bold, Indian-like design will work out best. Spray the finished painting with clear varnish or plastic to make it more durable. When these are mounted on a background of burlap-covered board, they can be framed and hung.

Seaweed Prints

This needs careful, neat work, but when the print is finished it will look like a very delicate watercolor sketch, well worth framing.

Take a bucket to the beach, especially after a storm or very high tide. Fill it with clear salt water. Then try to find some specimen of seaweeds, especially those with pretty, red, brown, yellow or green colors, and with not-too-wide fronds. Look in any little salt-water pools for specimens that might be trapped there. Take them home, and separate them from each other by hand, being careful not to break them. Keep the hands under water while doing this. Remove every bit of sand, soil, or other foreign objects.

While the seaweeds are still in the water, gently lower a sheet of paper (drawing paper or typing paper is good). Move it around under the water until it is under one of the seaweeds. Then raise it gently, tilting it just enough to let the water run off. Before the water is all off, maneuver the seaweed into a graceful design on the paper. Then place the paper on a flat surface and let it dry. The seaweed will stick to the paper with its own juices. You will have a lovely print.

White or very light paper works best. Try mounting the little print against a dark green background. Two or three of these prints in similar frames make a lovely wall grouping.

Driftwood

Driftwood is a real treasure. Collected and dried out it makes fire for a beach cookout, for one thing. If small pieces are collected and put into plastic or net bags, they make nice Christmas gifts for friends with fireplaces because they add lovely colors to the flames. Best of all, however, driftwood can be used in all sorts of lovely craft projects.

Sometimes flat pieces of driftwood, torn from planks or boxes, or other wooden objects, can be found. These are often bleached almost white by the sun and salt, and have beautiful swirls worn into their surfaces by the action of the waves. Often the surface has been worn as soft as silk, and has a lovely texture. Sometimes they have the added interest of being pitted with wormholes in interesting patterns. Pieces of this sort make marvellous backgrounds for shell pictures and plaques as described earlier in this Part. They often are just the right size to sit on small easels, or plate holders, or oriental stands from a gift shop. Decorated with shell pictures, they make lovely and unusual decorations for tables, shelves and mantel.

A large piece of driftwood, especially when it has once been the trunk or roots of a tree, gets rubbed by sand, wind and waves into a strange and wonderful shape. Sometimes animals, or birds, or human forms seem captured in the wood. Sometimes the shape is free-form and graceful.

It is a good idea to bring back some of these larger pieces, and study them to discover the forms latent in them. Set them up on a porch or patio where you will pass by often. Look at them from all angles. Suddenly you will see the hidden shape, and can help it to emerge.

In preparing driftwood, any broken splinters should be broken off and/or sanded. Any soft or rotten places should be cut out. Usually small pieces will need nothing but a brushing with a soft brush to remove sand. Too much scrubbing or hard brushing might remove some of the lovely patina given by sun and salt.

Larger pieces may need a good rubbing and brushing. Some may even need a good bath. Sometimes a piece may need a sanding to remove rough edges, or to bring out a latent shape. A good general rule is to do as little to driftwood as possible. It is beautiful in itself, and always loses its innate quality of charm when it is painted gold or silver, or distorted into unnatural forms.

Driftwood Sculpture can be used for table and wall decorations. Sometimes interesting shapes can be made into lamp bases—in which case, the lamp shades should be as simple as possible, so as not to detract from the beauty of the wood. Smaller bits of driftwood can be treasured as adjuncts to flower arranging, and to make into interesting free-form jewelry.

Driftwood is not necessarily limited to beaches. It can sometimes be found in woods and along streams. Sometimes the roots of an uprooted tree take on interesting forms. Sometimes a limb of a fallen tree is shaped in a graceful free-form. Wood from woods and streams, however, has not had the curing given beach driftwood and may need to be well-scrubbed and examined for soft places which should be removed. Bark from such wood should also be removed, since it is likely to harbor beetles and is quick to dry out, fall off, or decay.

Fish Print

When someone brings in his or her first fish—or an especially fine one—make a record of it. Take a photograph, yes, but after that make an honest-to-goodness fish print before it is skinned and eaten.

It's a bit messy, but the print can turn out to be amazingly

120

lovely. The Japanese have developed it into a real art form. With a soft brush, paint one side of the fish lightly all over with a vegetable dye or water color. Then, with great care, put a piece of white tissue paper down on the painted side of the fish, and rub it carefully, to bring out the designs of the scales. Then let the tissue paper dry out on a flat surface. If it is too wrinkled, iron it with a warm iron.

If you like the result, and want to try it again in a more expert way, buy some sheets of Japanese rice paper, and use them instead of the tissue. Mount the print against a contrasting color of paper, and frame. You'll be surprised at how pretty this print will be.

Starfish or Sand Dollar Preservation

Children are fascinated by these strange objects and heartbroken when they break so easily. They can be made quite a bit more permanent—at least enough to get home to the Beach Treasure Box, by a very simple step.

Make sure that the starfish or sand dollar is dead and thoroughly dry. Brush off any sand or other debris. Then spray it with a clear shellac. You'll be surprised at how much stronger they will become—and will look lovely as well.

How SALTY the Sea?

Yes, sea water is salty, but perhaps the child would like to know *how* salty. Make salt and see! Boil a cupful of seawater until only the salt is left. How much is there? Measure it. It may be a teaspoonful!

Beach Treasure Box

Every child collects pretty beach findings and wants to take them home. Sometimes there must be a limit set, however, on the amount that can be taken home after a beach holiday or trip. A Beach Treasure Box may help save the day.

Let him make it for himself, out of a cigar box, or other wooden box. A round cheese box can be used nicely. The bottom should be covered with a mixture of glue and water, then a nice soft layer of cotton put on it to provide a soft base for treasures. Paint the inside of the top, or glue a pretty beach scene onto it. Provide another blanket of cotton for the child to put on top of his treasures as he fills his box. Paint the outside of the box in the child's favorite color, and put his name or initials on it.

Then it is up to him to find and to select what he wants to put into his beach treasure chest. It will be hard to choose, but the size of the box will limit the amount to those treasures that he simply *cannot* leave behind.

121

PART VII

Crafts From Nature's Indoor Magic

Something To Look For

The home is full of materials which, when combined, will give special effects or make something entirely new. Look for everyday things like laundry blueing, sand, salt, flour, household ammonia, soapflakes, sawdust, various paints, enamels and other coloring agents.

Look for the opportunity to *surprise* children—to mystify them, to arouse their interest and curiosity.

Look for new ways to make modeling materials, fingerpaints, soap bubbles. They are easy to make but expensive to buy. And the *making* of them becomes a project, to be followed by the new project of *using* them.

Something To Talk About

Talk about the magic of cooking—how many different ingredients can be combined to make something that looks and tastes entirely different from any one of the ingredients. What makes a soufflé rise? What makes dough rise? What is searing? What does it do to meat? What is salt? Where does it come from? Sugar?

Talk about *food*. Talk about the words that describe how food looks, smells, tastes. Talk about how food is cooked. Look at the oven thermometer and see how it works. Look at the timer. How does *it* work?

Talk about where food comes from (See Part IV). Talk about those far-away places, and the people who live in them. Talk about the ways by which food reaches the table from the time it is grown to the time it is eaten. What means of transportation are involved?

Talk about ways of keeping records of things. Talk about sketching and painting as ways to remember a walk, a trip, a holiday. Make miniature models out of homemade modeling clay. Learn the right names for things, and use them. Talk about the weather—and how it is forecasted. Watch the clouds, smoke from the chimneys, the branches of trees, the behavior of animals. Talk about how to read the weather maps in the daily paper. Make a simple little rain forecaster. Talk about how to read a thermometer, a barometer.

The kitchen is one of the best laboratories a child will ever know. Add a home workshop to the kitchen, and any child can learn the rudiments of chemistry and physics—the play way that can lead into new interests and hobbies if given encouragement.

Something To Make

There are many interesting projects that depend upon certain mixtures, or chemical reactions. Some are just-for-fun. Others have some specific results, such as the bronzing of green leaves, the making of a weather forecaster. All are quite simple, and require ingredients that are either usually present in the home, or can be bought at a local drugstore. Some are decorative, some mystifying. All are projects that will intrigue children and adults.

Coal Garden

This project has been given many names, such as Coal Plant, and Depression Plant. There are many recipes for making it, all quite similar, usually varying mainly in the amounts used. Many of them originally called for a lump of coal or coke, and this can still be used. In the modern day of oil and electric heat, however, it is often very hard to find a lump of coal!

A broken brick, a porous rock—even a synthetic sponge can be substituted for that lump of coal. Whatever is used, it should be soaked in water until it is thoroughly wet. In the case of the sponge, squeeze it out.

Then place the object in a shallow glass or bowl—no metal. If you like, work out a little scene with twigs, miniature figures, and the like.

Then in a glass jar, make a mixture:

4 tablespoons of water
4 tablespoons of liquid blueing, the old-fashioned kind
4 tablespoons of household ammonia

Pour this mixture over the coal, brick, rock or sponge, making it thoroughly wet. Add a drop of food coloring, if you like. And for contrast, a drop of blueing in a corner.

Then sprinkle four tablespoons of salt over the coal, brick, rock or sponge. In a few hours, crystals will start to form and will grow—and grow—and grow! In about two days, they will have taken on weird forms.

When it stops growing and begins to dry out, add two more tablespoons of water and two tablespoons of ammonia, but *add them to the bowl, not the crystals.* The design will continue to grow. Follow this procedure every two days until the crystal formation is the size you want, but don't let the crystals grow over the rim of the glass or bowl. They will disfigure the table. Wipe off the rim of the glass or bowl with a paper towel if the crystals start forming on it.

As the design dries it gets crumbly. To preserve it as a centerpiece, or conversation piece, invert a glass bowl over it.

Dancing Snowballs

Another mystifying and entertaining project, fun to make—and fun to watch and talk about.

Fill a glass bowl (a goldfish bowl is perfect) about three-quarters full of water, *measuring the water.* Add about four or five mothballs per cup of water used. Add a drop or two of green, blue, or red coloring, if you like.

Place the bowl where spattering won't hurt anything—perhaps on a counter, or in the sink. Then add, slowly, one-third cup of white vinegar and one teaspoon of *moist* baking soda for each cup of water used. This mixture will fizz up, but when it stops fizzing the mothballs will start dancing up and down in a most mystifying manner.

When they slow down, re-activate them by adding another half-teaspoon of moist soda for each cup of water. Use as a centerpiece, or conversation piece. Fun!

Weather Prophet

It is easy to add a magic touch to weather forecasting. Youngsters can make this little forecaster, based on the same principle as the little German toy in which a girl in a pink dress, or a boy in a blue suit, pops out to forecast the weather. Such an instrument depends upon a chemical solution. White cotton cloth or paper toweling that has been immersed in this solution can be used to make a flag on a toy house, a sail on a toy boat, clothes for sketched figures, or a tail for an animal—a donkey is one of the favorites.

The solution requires these ingredients, some available from the local drugstore:

> 4 oz. of water
> 1 oz. of chloride of cobalt
> ½ oz. of table salt

¼ oz. of gum arabic

75 grains of calcium chloride

Immerse the cloth or toweling in this solution, then allow to dry out. It will turn pink in rainy, stormy weather, be blue in good weather.

Rock Candy

Rock candy is made by sugar crystallizing around a string. It is like magic. Children will enjoy seeing it work—then eating the result.

All you need is a cup of water and one and three-quarters cups of granulated sugar. Boil the water, take it off the heat and stir in the sugar. Add a drop or two of food coloring if you want to make colored crystal candy. Let the solution cool. Then pour it into a glass jar that has *been heated well.*

Tie a string around a pencil, and tie a nail or other small weight to the other end of the string, making the length of the string the same as the height of the glass jar. Place the pencil across the top of the jar so that the string hangs straight down into the jar of the sugar water.

The mixture will need to stand for several days. The water will gradually evaporate, and as it does the sugar crystals will form around the string. Don't move or jar the glass during the crystallizing process. Look but don't touch!

Invisible Writing

Very simple, but young G-Men will like sending invisible notes to each other. Just put lemon juice (the real thing), into a dish or small jar. Use an old-fashioned nibbed pen, or anything sharp, even a toothpick. Write the message by dipping it into the lemon juice and writing on a piece of notepaper or typing paper. Let the lemon juice dry. The message will be invisible.

BUT—hold the message over a candle, light bulb, or other source of heat, and out pops the writing in a brown color. The lemon juice has the property of changing color when heated.

Soap Bubbles

Any eight-to-one mixture of soap flakes and water will make good bubbles, but for SUPER bubbles that are strong and colorful, use this mixture:

1 cup of distilled water

⅛ cup of soap flakes

½ cup of glycerin

Stir the soap into the water until it is completely dissolved. Add a drop or so of food coloring if you like, and the glycerin. Let the mixture stand for an hour. Skim off any surface bubbles with a spoon, or the edge of a paper towel. Pour the mixture into a jar and use as needed.

Try using different things to blow bubbles—the edge of a funnel, a soda straw, a spool. A pleasant activity for a hot day.

Sand Clay

Another modeling medium, inexpensive and useful.

> 1 cup of sand
> ½ cup of cornstarch
> ½ cup of boiling water
> Food coloring as desired.

Mix the sand and cornstarch well. Pour in the boiling water and food coloring. Cook until the mixture is thick, stirring constantly. Let cool.

When cool, model this mixture into small animals, birds, butterflies, beads or other objects. To dry, bake in an oven set at 300 degrees for an hour, or until the articles are dry.

Shellac or paint the finished items if you like, after they are dry and cold.

Salt Ceramics

This is an inexpensive but useful "dough" that can be modeled into small objects, or molded into beads. It is somewhat similar to the Salt-and-Flour Flowers mixture described in Part V, but is made a bit differently.

Mix the following ingredients in the top of a double boiler:

> 1 cup of table salt
> ¾ cup of cold water
> ½ cup of cornstarch

Cook this mixture over heat, stirring constantly. When it gets as stiff as bread dough, drop it onto waxed paper and let it cool. Knead it with the hands for several minutes. Then mold it into whatever objects you want. If you are making beads, stick holes into each bead after you have rolled it in your palms so that the beads may be strung.

This mixture will dry very hard, and can be painted.

Glamorizing Artificial Flowers for Flower Arrangements

Sometimes when real flowers are hard to get, or are very expensive, artificial ones can be used for flower arranging. These often look *so* artificial! They can be given a new and more glamorous look by treating them as follows:

Mix equal parts of light oak varnish and turpentine. Add powdered gold (gilt) or silver (aluminum) so that it makes a film on top of the mixture. A teaspoonful will give a soft edging to several sprays.

Dip the flower or spray of flowers into the mixture, holding the stem and lowering the flower into and out of the mixture. Shake off the excess by putting them into a large paper bag, and holding the stems by the top of the bag. Hang the bag up by tying a string around the top, so the flowers can drip and then dry out, hanging upside down.

When the flowers are dry, they have somewhat of a Victorian look, and the petals will have a slight edging of the gilt or silver color. Arrange them in a pretty flower vase or bowl.

Bronzing Leaves

Sometimes in making Thanksgiving and Christmas decorations out of broad-leaved evergreens, such as magnolia leaves or laurel leaves, bronzed leaves would make a nice contrast. They are easy to make.

Just put the stems of the leaf branches into a vase, in a mixture of two parts water to one part glycerin. Let the stems stay in this mixture for two weeks, and the leaves will take on a very handsome bronzy color.

Frosted Glass

A simple way to decorate a glass or vase for a holiday or other occasion.

Add epsom salts to a saucepan holding two cupfuls of boiling water until no more of the salts will dissolve—in other words, you will have a saturated solution. Add a few drops of liquid glue to help make the "frost" adhere to the glass.

Then with a brush apply the mixture to the outside of the glass or vase in whatever design you like—all-over frosting, holly leaves, initials, and the like. The liquid will begin to evaporate almost at once, and the crystals of the salts will look just like frost but can be washed off.

To Flameproof Costumes

Every year newspapers carry stories of children burned to death or seriously injured because their costumes caught fire from lanterns, candles, open fireplace, or other source. Here is a simple way to prevent this.

Mix nine ounces of borax and four ounces of boric acid in a gallon of water. Dip the costumes into this mixture, wring them out by hand, and hang the costume to dry. Repeat this process after each laundering.

127

Resources

Books

Abbott, R. Tucker. *Seashells of the World.* (A Golden Nature Guide.) New York: Simon and Schuster, 1962

Bale, Robert O. *Stepping Stones to Nature* and *Creative Nature Crafts.* Minneapolis, Minn.: Burgess Publishing Co., 1960 and 1959

Fischer, Helen Field and Harshbarger, Gretchen Fischer. *Flower Family Album.* Minnesota: University of Minnesota Press, 1941

Grimm, William Cary. *Book of Trees.* Harrisburg, Pa.: Stackpole Books, 1962

———— *Recognizing Flowering Wild Plants.* Harrisburg, Pa.: Stackpole Books, 1968

Ickis, Marguerite. *Nature In Recreation,* rev. ed. New York: A. S. Barnes and Co., 1965

Peterson, Roger Tory. *A Field Guide To the Birds.* New York: Houghton Mifflin Co., 1934

Sterling, Dorothy. *The Story of Mosses, Ferns and Mushrooms.* New York: Doubleday and Co., 1955

Teale, Edwin Way. *Junior Book of Insects.* New York: E. P. Dutton, 1953

van der Smissen, Betty and Goering, Oswald H. *A Leader's Guide To Nature Oriented Activities.* Ames: Iowa State University Press, 1965

Magazines

Natural History, published by the American Museum of Natural History, Central Park West at 79 St., New York, N.Y. 10024. Monthly

Nature and Science, published by the American Museum of Natural History, Central Park West at 79 St., New York, N.Y. 10024. Fortnightly

Organizations

American Museum of Natural History, Central Park West at 79 St., New York, N.Y. 10024

Audubon Society, 1130 Fifth Avenue, New York, N.Y. 10028

Boy Scouts of America, New Brunswick, N.J. 08903

Camp Fire Girls, 65 Worth Street, New York, N.Y. 10013

Cornell University Press, 124 Roberts Place, Ithaca, N.Y. 14850

Girl Scouts of the USA, 830 Third Avenue, New York, N.Y. 10022

National Recreation and Park Association, 1700 Pennsylvania Avenue, N.W., Washington, D.C. 20006

National Wildlife Federation, 1412 16 Street, N.W., Washington, D.C. 20036